40
days in

1 CORINTHIANS

Titles in 40 Days Series

1 CORINTHIANS

HERSHAEL W. YORK

— *edited by* —

WILLIAM F. COOK III

B&H
PUBLISHING
NASHVILLE, TENNESSEE

Published by B&H Publishing Group
Nashville, Tennessee

Dewey Decimal Classification: 242.5
Subject Heading: DEVOTIONAL LITERATURE / BIBLE. N.T.
1 CORINTHIANS—STUDY AND TEACHING /
CHRISTIAN LIFE

Cover illustration by SweetRenie/shutterstock

1 2 3 4 5 6 • 24 23 22 21

Contents

Preface

Forty is an important number in the Bible. Moses was on Mount Sinai with the Lord God for forty days (Exod. 34:28), Elijah traveled for forty days before arriving at Mount Horeb (1 Kings 19:3–8), and Jesus was tempted in the wilderness for forty days (Mark 1:13). Some self-help experts believe it takes forty days to develop a habit. Whether they're right or wrong, there is no habit more important for a Christian to develop than a consistent devotional life.

In *40 Days in the Word*, readers will discover a humble attempt to assist believers longing for a fresh moving of God's Spirit in their life. This series intends to enable believers to read through books of the Bible in their devotional time discovering God's truth within its biblical context. The Spirit of God uses the Word of God to mature believers in their faith and increase their passion and zeal for Jesus Christ.

Many Christians find it difficult to sustain momentum in their devotional life. They desire to read the Bible consistently but lack encouragement, guidance, and direction. Commentaries are often too technical, and devotionals may fail to challenge them to dig deeply into God's Word. The *40 Days* series offers both a deeper discussion of a biblical passage and at the same time encourages the reader to make personal application based upon what the text *actually* says.

We live in a day where casual Christianity (which is not biblical Christianity at all!) has infected the church in the West. People are clamoring for shorter sermons that are more focused on felt-needs rather than on the Bible, and many in the pulpits are obliging. Furthermore, the songs that are often sung fail to extol the greatness of God, but instead make people feel better about themselves and their comfortable lifestyles.

If the church in the West is to recapture the passion of the early church, God's people must spend time on their knees with their Bibles open allowing God's Spirit to convict them of their sin, build them up in their faith, and empower them to take the gospel across the street and around the world. The hope of the authors of this series is that God's Spirit will use these volumes to help God's people develop an ever-increasing love for their Savior, Jesus Christ.

In addition to helping individual believers, the series holds out hope for small groups desiring to focus their meetings on the study of the Bible. A group would spend approximately two months (five days of readings per week) reading through a book of the Bible along with the *40 Days* volume, and then base their discipleship time encouraging each other with what they discovered during the previous week.

The Spirit of God and the Word of God work together to strengthen God's church. The apostle Paul put it this way: "Let the word of Christ dwell richly among you, in all wisdom teaching and admonishing one another through psalms, hymns, and spiritual songs, singing to God with gratitude in your hearts" (Col. 3:16). Paul's hope is my prayer for you as you journey through these next forty days.

Bill Cook
Holy Week, 2020

Being a Saint in a Sinful World

1 Corinthians 1:1–9

The Big Picture

Acts 18 gives an account of Paul's eighteen months in the city of Corinth during which time he grew a deep relationship with the members of the young church planted there. Through correspondence and emissaries, he had maintained a close, if somewhat rocky, relationship with them ever since his departure. Though this letter is named "First" Corinthians, Paul's words in 1 Corinthians 5:9–13 confirm at least one earlier letter he had sent. References to a letter from them are sprinkled throughout this epistle as well. Learning that they had departed from the solid doctrinal foundation he had laid, Paul urgently composed his answer to deal with the many divisions, errors, and outright sins that permeated the church. Paul begins his letter with great irony, therefore, by calling the Corinthians "saints." Sainthood is not bestowed upon super-Christians with holy behavior, but upon all who have trusted in Christ and are "sanctified in Christ Jesus" (1:2). Paul is making the point that those who are in Christ should also *act* like saints—even in a wicked world and a sensual society. Many historians describe Corinth as a city of unbridled passion and sexual orgies, basing their view on certain remarks of ancient writers. Though Paul's letter specifically addresses the many problems in the Corinthian church, this book is really about *holiness*, about living the Christian life. In fact, if we wanted to distill all of Paul's church epistles into a single grand truth, it would be this: ***act like what you are***. The Corinthians, like their twenty-first-century counterparts, did not need to learn how to be righteous, but rather how to *live out* the righteousness that Christ has provided, even when immersed in a culture that is decidedly unholy.

Digging In

Apart from his salvation, the key to Paul's self-understanding is his apostleship (1:1). Perhaps the most astounding truth that Paul delivers is this precious reminder of what the Corinthian believers are and what God expects of them. The phrase is literally expressed, "called holy" or "called saints." One might wonder if the apostle has suffered from either amnesia or dementia. Divisions, fornication, doctrinal aberration, theological misunderstandings, and irregular practice pervaded the congregation. All these things together added up to a church with sin, schisms, and sorrows. Yet Paul called them "sanctified" and "saints."

Sanctification is not some magical infused holiness that makes temptation evaporate. Sanctification means to be set apart, designated for God's purpose through the person and work of Christ. Though they are in Corinth, they can be holy because they are also "in Christ Jesus."

Paul ends the verse by giving his readers a second truth that can help them as they seek to lead holy lives. They are not in this struggle alone! The apostle reminds them that the truth in his letter applies also to "those in every place who call on the name of Jesus Christ our Lord" (1:2). Christians all over the world over are united by faith in Christ, regardless of race, class, economic status, or anything else that might divide. He is "their Lord and ours."

Paul's prayer for the Corinthians (1:3) is very similar to his invocation in several of his other epistles (Rom. 1:7; Gal. 1:3; Eph. 1:2). This grace for which he prays is not merely a meaningless formulaic expression. He is grateful for the grace of God that has already been given to them, a grace that has enriched them and brought them many wonderful benefits in Christ.

In light of his later words of rebuke and correction, Paul's pastoral wisdom here is stunning. He expresses delight that they don't lack *any* gifts (1 Cor. 1:7). Tucked in Paul's encouragement is the assurance that Jesus will enable the Corinthians to persevere. They demonstrated their giftedness as the testimony of Christ was "confirmed" among them (1:6), a word that means "to guarantee or verify."[1] The result is that just as the gospel was "confirmed" in them by their giftedness, so Jesus will "confirm" (translated "strengthen" in 1:8) them to the end. God's purpose in doing this is to make them "blameless" on the day of the Lord Jesus Christ (1:8). Elsewhere Paul wrote that God "chose us in him, before the foundation of the world, to be holy and *blameless* in love before him" (Eph. 1:4, italics added). Significantly, Paul did not say that we will ever be *faultless*, but that we will be *blameless*. We will always have a sinful past, but the scars of Jesus will bear witness that God does not hold our sin against us.

Despite all the sin in the church and its members, Paul reminds them of the faithfulness of God (1 Cor. 1:9). He is always faithful. The same God by whom "you were called . . . into fellowship with his Son, Jesus Christ our Lord" is the faithful God who "will strengthen you to the end." Three times in these introductory verses Paul uses the word *called*. He is called to be an apostle (1:1); the Corinthians are called saints (1:2); and they have been called into fellowship with Jesus Christ (1:9).

Interestingly, after assuring his readers of their security in Christ who will keep them blameless, Paul immediately reminds them that there is more to the Christian life than basking in their security. God called them into *fellowship*, not complacency.

Living It Out

This passage has wide-reaching implications for life. Paul teaches that believers can and must be holy, even when immersed in a culture that is not. Paul's choice of the word *saint* to identify believers is both a reminder and a subtle rebuke. **"Act like what you are"** is his challenge. Believers should remember Paul's declaration that, during this period in which we wait for the Lord's return, the church not lack any spiritual gift (1:7). No matter how inadequate we may feel, no matter how much we have struggled, our failures are not because we are not equipped. In Jesus we obtained everything needed for life and godliness (2 Pet. 1:3). When you feel weak, you can be strong, for we know *he* keeps *us*—*we* don't keep ourselves. Our security is rooted, not in our service, but in our Savior. We can be strong, we can endure, we can persevere! If Paul could make this promise to first-century Christians in Corinth with all of their problems and sins, twenty-first-century Christians can believe it too.

The overwhelming encouragement of the entire passage is that salvation is of the Lord! God is faithful, even when we are not. God graciously calls us into fellowship with his Son. God enriches us and gifts us by the grace given us in his Son, which motivates and enables us to be saints—to be *holy*—*even* in a sinful world.

Dealing with Divisions

1 Corinthians 1:10–17

The Big Picture

A lengthy list of problems needed confrontation and correction in the Corinthian congregation, but Paul had to deal with the biggest problem first. Before he dealt with fornication, or church discipline, lawsuits, the ordinances, marriage, sex, food offered to idols, gender issues, tongues, prophecy, or even their denial of the resurrection, he had to deal with *division in the church.*

Disagreements are inevitable, but they are compounded in churches that neglect the basics. Churches that forget evangelism and discipleship lose their way. Each member casts his own vision and follows his own direction for the church. The result may be tremendous energy, but almost no productivity.

Paul's priority must be the urgency of churches today. Unity around the person and gospel of Jesus Christ is essential to fulfill God's purpose. Paul's words still ring true and provide a blueprint for dealing with disagreements and divisions in the church.

Digging In

In order to have unity, a church needs a unifying principle, a source of fellowship by which each member can be united to all others. Paul reveals the key by the way he bases his appeal on the name and authority of the Lord Jesus Christ (1 Cor. 1:10). In Jewish thought, invoking someone's name appropriated that person's power and personality, so the messenger had to be heard and obeyed as if the one who sent him were personally asking.[2] His request has three parts, but the first and third say the same thing. First, he asks simply that they "agree in what you say." Next, he requests that, as a result of their agreement, there should "be no divisions among" them. Finally, he desires that they be "united with the same understanding and the same conviction."

The church at Corinth was like a team on which each player listened to a favorite assistant coach, but no one paid attention to the head coach. The apostle had information that the church at Corinth was quarrelling, and to make matters worse, the arguments in the church were not about doctrine or mission strategy, but were centered on personalities and pious pretension. Rather than a common commitment to the gospel, they were interested in individual inclinations. They were focused on at least four personalities: Paul, Apollos, Peter, and Christ (1:11–12). Why these four? While no one can be sure, clues found throughout the New Testament suggest possibilities. Perhaps some identified with Paul, a personality of Christian *liberty*. Others were drawn to Apollos, a personality of *learning* (Acts 18:24–28). Apollos was an Alexandrian Jew, educated in the center of secular scholarship, yet mighty in his understanding of Holy Scripture. A third group of believers in the church felt a connection with Peter, a personality of *law*. Paul's use of his Hebrew name, Cephas, suggests that some of the Jewish believers in Corinth may have found the freedom of Paul and even the knowledge of Apollos beyond their comfort zone. Peter represented Judea, the temple, the law, which offered some familiarity and a comfort about his connections to Judaism. A fourth group seems surely to have gotten it right because they claimed that they were of Christ! No human personalities sufficed for these pious theologians! If they really meant it, however, Paul would have commended them.

No one can be sure what they meant. Perhaps they were attracted to a personality of *love*—not the true love of Christ, but a syrupy, indulgent emotion devoid of standards. Whatever reasons they used to justify their identification with Christ, they were not the right ones.

Paul immediately launches a rhetorical barrage at the factions in Corinth, challenging them to remember to *whom* they are called. "Is Christ divided? Was Paul crucified for you? Or were you baptized in the name of Paul?" (1 Cor. 1:13). The obvious answer to each question is an emphatic "no." Paul's advice has a simple meaning: *don't follow anyone without nail prints in his hands.* Only Jesus died, was buried, rose, and ascended, and only he has called us.

If Paul's reminder of the one who called them is a rebuke, so is his remark about the nature of baptism. One cannot deny Paul's high view of baptism. In Romans 6:3 he explains baptism is identification with Christ. Believers baptized into Christ are baptized into his death. Baptism always means *identification*. If Jesus is the one who calls, identification with him and participation in him is the purpose of that calling. But for all of Paul's belief in baptism and even insistence on it for believers, this passage reads very differently.

Paul went so far as to say something that sounds shocking: "I thank God that I baptized none of you" (1 Cor. 1:14). Rather than being flattered that some of the Corinthians had identified with *him*, Paul felt incensed. Some Corinthian believers completely misunderstood the object of their identification. Even if he had baptized a few of them, the gospel was at the heart of his calling, not baptizing people or to show off his wisdom. Anything added to the gospel nullifies the gospel (1:17)!

Living It Out

Division occurs when we live by feelings rather than by faith, compare ourselves to others, and exaggerate the negative. All these mistakes are evident in the Corinthian church. But all these underlying causes have one solution: the proper use of their *minds*. If members will focus on their common concern—namely, the gospel of Jesus Christ—they

can overcome the division that often grows out of a diversity of experience, gifts, and personalities.

We tend to romanticize and idolize the people who point us to
Christ. Drawn to winsome personalities, we lose sight of the grace of
God that called and gifted them for service. The thing that divides the
world—"the message of the cross" (1:18 NIV)—must be the thing that
unites the church. True gospel preaching points to Christ, not to self.
True Christians identify with the Christ who is preached, not the one
who preaches.

The Word of the Cross

1 Corinthians 1:18–25

The Big Picture

What identifies the church? Some may assume that massive buildings, recreation halls, church officers, bank accounts, involved members, and educated clergy are the identifying marks. Such organizations can draw a pretty good crowd, create some excitement, distract attention from the cruel heat of life, and put on a very good show. The only problem is they lack the one thing essential for the church—the *gospel*.

This problem is not new. At the core of the Corinthian catastrophe was the crisis of the cross. In their admiration of personalities, they neglected the power of God. In response to their division, Paul pointed them to the unity of Christ (1 Cor. 1:13a), the meaning of their baptism (1:13b), and now he directs them to the heart of the gospel of Jesus Christ—the message and meaning of the cross. Only a clear understanding of the gospel can make the church enjoy lasting unity and fulfill its purpose. Even though it may seem foolish to the world that someone's death two thousand years ago can save anyone today, the church must keep the cross at the heart of its mission, or it will lose the gospel completely.

Digging In

God alone saves. And he saves through the "word of the cross" (1:18). The mention of the cross in verse 17 introduces a section of strange opposites. Paul pits the foolishness of man against the wisdom of God, a wisdom that cannot be naturally discerned. The power of God is displayed as greater than the weakness of man's wisdom. The message of the cross divides its audience. Paul contrasts the reaction of the lost and the saved, but not between "foolishness" and, what we would expect, "wisdom," but rather between "foolishness" and "power." The factions in the church at Corinth were obsessed with personalities: who is the smartest, the most capable, the most successful. Their great mistake was that they attempted to mix man's wisdom with God's revealed message.

God's wisdom is revealed primarily in the cross of Christ and, because the human mind is clouded by sin, is not naturally received. Through the cross, God fulfills his promise of Isaiah 29:14: "Therefore, I will again confound these people with wonder after wonder. The wisdom of their wise will vanish, and the perception of their perceptive will be hidden." Human wisdom leads to the conclusion that salvation is earned. Human intelligence makes people think that they can save themselves. But through the cross, God demonstrates his wrath, his justice, and humanity's complete inability to appease a God who hates sin.

God's plan of salvation establishes human inability. The scheme of salvation that God designed runs contrary to the human intuition and wisdom. People hate to admit either their sinfulness or their complete helplessness, yet the cross of Christ demands that they acknowledge both.

In his inscrutable wisdom, God designed the plan of salvation. The mind of God conceived a way in which his justice could be satisfied, the debt of sin could be paid, the righteousness of a sinner could be established, a relationship between God and the redeemed could be maintained, and God alone could receive glory. Only the cross meets all of these requirements. The cross is the ultimate representation of God's wisdom. And since humans, left to their own wisdom, could never understand that scheme, let alone devise it, God decided to save his people through the foolishness of preaching. Through this preaching, both in its activity and content, God saves those who believe.

While God's wisdom is revealed primarily in the cross, fallen humanity rejects God's wisdom and believes whatever the culture values (1 Cor. 1:22ff). Inherent in the message of the cross is the admission that human religion and effort is completely useless. Accepting Christ's cross entails rejecting everything that one has valued and pursued. Consequently, Paul mentions three possible reactions to the gospel message. The Jews considered the cross a *scandal.* Given their misunderstanding of the Messiah, they could not conceive of a Christ on a cross. A God who dies? A creator who is crucified? They would have expected a king on a throne, not a carpenter on a cross.

The Greeks, on the other hand, met the message with *scorn.* They saw no wisdom in the cross. Yet in the face of their scandal and scorn, Paul remains unintimidated and unashamed. Note the triumphant tone of his pen as he calls on the wise, the teacher, the debater (1:20). To all their objections Paul has only one reply: "we preach Christ crucified" (1:23).Paul knows that the third response is *acceptance.* This acceptance, however, is not because they are wise or because they receive a supernatural sign. They can see the power of God in the cross because they are *called* (1:24). The Spirit's calling enables and moves them to realize that the thing they have valued is worthless and that the cross is not foolishness, but rather the wisdom of God. The cross is not an obstacle, but rather their only opportunity to have forgiveness and a relationship with their Creator. God's calling is the only way people can abandon their own limited wisdom. Apart from the gracious intervention and call of God, no one could have hope.

Paul's words about the cross also operate on a deeper level, however. When Paul lists the things that the Jews and the Greeks value, he is addressing the Corinthian Christians as well. From the appearance of their factions and their problems with spiritual gifts, they had begun to relapse into their old way of thinking. The divisions indicate that they were focusing on personalities that represented the things their culture craved. Paul, Apollos, and Peter were all viewed with various degrees of human wisdom and even, at least in the apostles' case, supernatural signs. Paul's words about the cross's superiority is as much a rebuke to the Corinthians as theological formulation.

The Corinthian church had moved away from the message of the cross and was facing dire consequences as a result. Christ alone is "the power of God and the wisdom of God" (1:24). Even God's foolishness—the preaching of the cross—is better and wiser than the wisdom of the world, and God's weakness—Christ crucified—is stronger than any human effort at achieving a righteousness by works.

Living It Out

In a postmodern world that rejects absolutes, the cross of Christ dares to delineate distinctly between right and wrong, sin and righteousness, heaven and hell. In a world that glorifies pluralism, the cross boldly claims to be the exclusive means of salvation and a relationship with God. In a culture that avoids unpleasantries, the cross unambiguously confronts us with the heinous death and blood sacrifice of God's Son as the only means to satisfy God's wrath. The church of the twenty-first century faces the same danger as the church of the first century. We are tempted to pursue personalities rather than truth, to seek acceptance rather than obedience, to seem tolerant rather than convinced. Hearing the cross of Christ disparaged as a slaughter-house religion tempts us to make the death of Christ the church's dirty little secret. Better to talk about a babe in a manger than the Lamb of God on a tree. Better to portray him as the victim of an oppressive government's injustice than the object of his father's wrath. Better to laud him as a great ethical teacher than to worship him as the sinless Son of God. Yet the instant the church caves into culture and ignores the caveat of Paul, the church *forfeits* the power of God. The preaching of the cross always *divides* an audience. It cannot do otherwise. To some it is the odor of life that leads to life; and for others, it is the odor of death that leads to death. To some it is the wisdom of God, but to others it is the foolish imaginations of a human religion. But the cross is the means by which God saves his people, so it must be central not only to the church, but to every Christian. One cannot be saved by the wisdom of God and live by the wisdom of the world. The way of salvation is the way of sanctification, and both are through the cross.

The Insult of the Gospel

1 Corinthians 1:26–31

The Big Picture

Paul first established that the *message* God uses—the cross—is foolishness to men (1 Cor. 1:18), then he reminded them that the *method* God uses—preaching—is foolishness, also. Now he gets personal, perhaps even a little insulting. He points out that the *material* God chooses is equally unimpressive. God does everything for his own glory, and he is most glorified when only he can claim the glory and the credit for salvation. If God's own glory is his ultimate goal and motive, so should it be the same goal of the believer.

Digging In

In 1 Corinthians 1:26, Paul's bluntness shatters any grand notions the Corinthians may have had about themselves. If they presumed that they were doing God a favor by agreeing to be his people, Paul prescribed a bitter dose of reality. "Consider your calling," he urges them. When Jesus called them, he called them *out* of something. Paul's reminder keeps us in awe of God's grace. God reached down to save us because we could never reach up to him, much less save ourselves. Only when we let go of our own righteousness could we accept his. The message of the cross teaches that self-righteousness will keep us from heaven as much as sin.

Considering that God needs nothing in us, no foreseen merit that makes us attractive to him, we might wonder why he would ever forgive us and call us to himself. Paul answers that God has a program of self-glorification. His ultimate purpose is to display his glory throughout his creation. He does that most beautifully when he saves worthless sinners. The human heart rebels at both of these truths. We feel offended when Paul reminds us of our own estate, and we feel outraged at the notion of God glorifying himself. We have always been taught that it is rude to brag on oneself, to list one's own wonderful attributes, but that is because humans live in the realm of comparison and degrees of attributes. God, however, is superlative in all things. He has no equal and is perfect in all his ways. His self-glorification is not only permissible, but necessary! His glory is his sacred purpose in all he does from creation to the cross to consummation.

People who seem worthless to the world become God's means of glorifying himself. God's most beautiful buildings are crafted from defective materials. The trophies of grace that shine most brightly for him are those with no claim to their own glory.

Paul instructs the Corinthians that it is because of God that we are in Christ Jesus (1:30), implying two important truths. The first regards the *disposition of God*. God the Father is the initiator of salvation. Any notion of the Godhead as a wrathful Father appeased by a pleading Son, as though God saves only reluctantly, is wrongheaded if not blasphemous. Though there is no division in the Trinity, Paul portrays our salvation as originating in the mind of the Father and accomplished through the obedience of the Son. Because of *him*—of God the Father—we are in Christ Jesus.

The second implication of this grand declaration regards the *position of believers*. We are not merely accepted *by* God, we are accepted *in Christ*. On the eve of his crucifixion, Jesus prayed, "Father, I want those you have given me to be with me where I am, so that they will see my glory, which you have given me because you loved me before the world's foundation" (John 17:24). Elsewhere Paul wrote that God—again, note the subject—has made us "accepted *in the beloved*" (Eph. 1:6 NKJV, italics added). God's provision of his own Son as the means of salvation is the only way sin could be forgiven.

Since the human mind could never invent or grasp God's way of redemption, Jesus is God's wisdom incarnate. That which the world deems as foolish is the only way to be reconciled to God. Paul clearly defines this wisdom from God: righteousness, sanctification, and redemption (1 Cor. 1:30). In this way, God demonstrates his wisdom.

These three words each describe an aspect and a tense of salvation. **Righteousness** is required to be able to stand before God. Since our righteousness is as filthy rags, God supplied righteousness by imputing to us the righteousness of Christ. His righteousness accomplished our *justification*. **Sanctification** is the practical aspect of salvation. It refers to holiness, which is the natural state of the Christian life as the believer emulates the character of Christ. Jesus provided our righteousness, but he also modeled perfect holiness for us. This growth in holiness and likeness to his character is our *sanctification*. **Redemption** is the description of our ultimate salvation, not only from sin's penalty, but also from its very presence and power. Salvation will only be complete when Jesus puts all enemies under his feet. Redemption is our *assurance* of that victory.

Together these three concepts teach the three tenses of our salvation. Trusting Christ, we were justified and saved from sin's penalty. Growing in holiness, we are being saved from sin's power. When Jesus returns and completes our redemption, we will be saved from sin's very presence.

Living It Out

Like the Corinthians, we were of lowly estate when Christ called us, though our initial encounter with Christ may seem very different on the surface. Some people shed many tears when they come to faith, while others may experience a very intellectual consideration of the claims of Christ. Some were saved in a Christian home, while others were in a horribly sinful lifestyle. Some were down and out when they came to faith, while others were affluent and self-absorbed. The only thing that all believers' experiences have in common is that, accompanying their acceptance of Christ, they felt an overwhelming sense of their own worthlessness, sinfulness, and inadequacy. In fact, salvation is impossible without it. No one reaches for a life preserver if they believe they can swim fine on their own. No one can be saved until they first acknowledge they are lost.

Overwhelmed with the richness of God's provision, Paul rebukes the Corinthians even as he leads them in worship. They had been boasting in men—even in Paul—but how foolish that seems when the apostle explains the mighty acts of God in saving his people. God alone has saved by revealing the wisdom of his plan—our righteousness, holiness, and redemption—in Jesus Christ, his Son. If anyone feels inclined to boast, they can only boast in the Lord. Salvation is of the Lord, and of the Lord alone.

Paul's Philosophy of Preaching

1 Corinthians 2:1–5

The Big Picture

The Corinthian church had divided around intriguing and talented personalities, preachers whom the Spirit had used to instruct and guide them. Though a faction had formed around Paul, he was neither complimented by their confidence in him nor jealous of the others who had followers in the church. Paul emphasized that the problem was not *whom* they followed, but that they followed *anyone* other than Christ. In order to get his point across that their salvation and sanctification depended on *the Spirit* of God rather than on the *man* of God, Paul reminds them of their shared history. As he tells that story, Paul constructs a simple but effective philosophy of preaching that needs to be recovered in the twenty-first century.

Digging In

No doubt many of the recipients of Paul's letter first heard the gospel as a result of Paul's ministry. Warren Wiersbe points out "a beautiful parallel between Matthew 28:18–20 and Acts 18:1–11"[3] in the Great Commission and the description of how Paul fulfilled it when he came to Corinth. When Paul arrived and began speaking in a public setting, the locals could not help but notice that he did not conform to the conventions used by the roving rhetors to which they were accustomed. They all wanted to impress with their skill more than to impact with their truth.

Paul's manner was entirely different. He was nothing like the others. As he preached the clear, unadulterated gospel, the Holy Spirit applied it to hearts, making them alive toward God as they repented of their sin and trusted Christ. Through preaching empowered by the Spirit, the Corinthians believers had changed despite the absence in Paul's preaching of the qualities that had attracted and mesmerized them when other orators spoke.

By the time of this letter, several years have passed, and many of the Corinthian believers have lapsed back into their old way of thinking. Behind the divisions in the church lay a worldly way of thinking. In response, Paul rebukes them for idolizing men and reminds them that the power of the gospel comes from God alone.

Unlike the educated speakers of his day, Paul never claimed to be able to speak on more than one subject. To the contrary, he only had one message, the message of the cross of Christ (1 Cor. 2:1), because only that message was the power of God unto salvation (Rom. 1:18). Paul's limited subject matter was another distinction between him and any other speaker the Corinthians had heard. He did not rely on breadth of knowledge any more than he trusted in his own skill. Furthermore, his deep conviction about the cross fired a passion within him that sheer brilliance and natural talent can never artificially attain.

Though Paul's subject was limited to the gospel, the gospel itself is not limited to one subject. The message of the cross is expansive in its scope as Paul's letter to the Corinthians itself makes clear. This, too, distinguished Paul and his message from anything else the Corinthians had ever heard. Whatever subject the Corinthians brought up, Paul was not so concerned about that particular matter *per se* as much as how it related to the gospel. The gospel is the lens through which Paul addresses *everything*!

Paul then states "I came to you in weakness" (2:3). In the Greek world, "weakness" was contemptible and undermined effectiveness, but Paul sees it precisely the opposite way. There really is something *powerful* about *weakness*. As contradictory as it seems, that is precisely what the Lord told Paul: "My grace is sufficient for you, for my power is perfected in weakness" (2 Cor. 12:9a). In human weakness the glory of the Lord shines brilliantly. Once Paul understood that he stopped asking the Lord to remove his weakness and responded, "Therefore, I will most gladly boast all the more about my weaknesses, so that Christ's power may reside in me. So I take pleasure in weaknesses, insults, hardships, persecutions, and in difficulties, for the sake of Christ. For when I am weak, then I am strong" (2 Cor. 12:9b–10).

Some have suggested that Paul is speaking primarily of his physical weaknesses due to the hardships of life he had experienced. Still, others suggest that Paul is referring primarily to the intimidation he felt as he considered the daunting task of preaching. He trembled at the knowledge of the eternal consequences of the preaching event. No doubt he experienced a combination of both. Weakness of body acutely reminds us of our dependence on God and our true inability to accomplish anything of worth in our own strength.

Had Paul trusted in his own skill as a speaker to persuade them, he would only have talked the Corinthians into something that anyone could talk them out of. Though Paul believed in being persuasive (see 2 Cor. 5:11), he wanted his persuasiveness to emanate from the Spirit of God, for only then would the results last because they belong to the Spirit as well. He did not rely on "persuasive words of wisdom" but instead his preaching was "with a demonstration of the Spirit's power" (1 Cor. 2:4). That "demonstration of the Spirit's power" was not some miraculous deed, but rather in the conviction and passion with which Paul preached, the conviction wrought in their hearts by the Holy Spirit, and the lives that changed as a result of that process.

Living It Out

Implicit in Paul's remark to know nothing except Christ crucified is the cross's claim on every aspect of the Christian's life. No quarter of existence, no field of endeavor, no aspect of humanity lies beyond the cross's reach or claim. The message of the cross is simple and comprehensive. Without the message of the cross, a preacher says nothing, no matter how many words are spoken.

We can be guilty of focusing on only a part of Jesus and conscripting him for our own purposes. Jesus in the manger is a safe religious symbol. Jesus feeding the hungry is caring. Jesus' leadership principles will help people achieve their goals. Jesus cleansing the temple can be used to claim that he hated "organized religion." One can find many ways to keep Jesus palatable and inoffensive. The cross, on the other hand, is not spoken about in polite company. What an offense! What a scandal that God would demand the death of his own Son in order to save sinners. Unfortunately, even some who claim to be his followers find that terribly offensive. They want a crossless Christ.

But for the great apostle, nothing could ever be more relevant, more encompassing, more essential for his listeners than the message that Jesus Christ died for the sins of all who will believe. When God spoke to Paul and encouraged him to stay in Corinth, he did so by telling him that he had many people in that city (Acts 18:10). Paul knew that the message those people needed was the message of the cross.

Much about human culture has changed since the first century, but not much about humans. Humanity's deepest need is no different, and neither is God's method of meeting that need. Every person is a sinner and separated from his or her infinitely holy Creator. A just God still demands that every sin be punished, either through eternal punishment in hell, or in the infinite God-man on the cross. It may not be palatable, but it is powerful.

The Effect of Our Preaching

1 Corinthians 2:6–9

The Big Picture

If preaching is foolishness to men, what can it accomplish? If, as Paul has just testified, he cannot rely on intellect or education but must rely on the Spirit's power, what does such preaching accomplish? In the remaining verses of chapter 2, Paul moves his audience into thinking about what that preaching *does*. Though he does not mention preaching explicitly, these words are part of the immediately preceding context and cannot be divorced from the larger discussion. He wants them to know what preaching Christ crucified accomplishes, how they can discern it, and the difference it will make in their lives. Specifically, Paul focuses on several things that this kind of cross-centered preaching accomplishes, and in each case, Paul shows how the preaching of the cross of Christ *always* divides the audience between two possible results.

Digging In

Paul underscores that this wisdom is completely different from the wisdom the world values (1 Cor. 2:6). Not only is Paul indoctrinating his original readers so that they have a solid understanding of the way God saves his people, but he is also laying the foundation for his continuing case against their factionalism, pride, and fawning praise of men. Properly understood, the grace of God in salvation precludes selfishness and sinfulness, petty divisions and proud distinctions. So long as the church relies on the world's wisdom, she is doomed to internecine squabbling and differences that overwhelm her fellowship in Christ. God's wisdom, however, is what unites everyone behind the cross and the mission it mandates for the Lord's church.

First, this wisdom **originates with God** (2:7). In other words, as Paul has frequently said, this wisdom is beyond man's mere rational ability. It can be understood by trusting children, yet it can confound the most educated man because it emanates from the divine mind.

Second, God's wisdom **has been hidden** (2:7). When Paul says "mystery," he means something that was previously hidden that is now revealed. A mystery in the Scripture is a divine purpose hidden in the counsels of God in the past but finally disclosed in a new revelation of God's redemptive work in Christ.[4] Before Jesus came as the perfect revelation of God, no one could have predicted that God would reveal his purpose and plan of salvation in such a way.

Third, this wisdom **has been planned** (2:7). Redemption was not an afterthought or even a divine reaction to the fall and sinfulness of man. God did not come up with a Plan B when Israel rejected Jesus and crucified him. God destined this wisdom for us before time began. Prior to Adam's sin and the fall of the human race, God "predestined" this wisdom "before the ages" (2:7).

Fourth, this wisdom **has a purpose** (2:7). Though God's ultimate purpose is to glorify himself, he has also determined to share his glory with his people. Paul is teaching the Corinthians that their glorying in men is not only sinful, it is *impractical*.

Fifth, this wisdom **will not be received by everyone** (2:8). The rulers of this age did not receive God's wisdom. They sought to extinguish the Light of the World, but their actions only fulfilled the eternal purpose of God and made him shine more brightly. If the rulers of this world had known that their crucifixion of Christ would have exalted him rather than extinguish him, surely, they would not have done it. Yet even their wicked actions were a part of God's premundane plan.

Finally, this wisdom **reveals God's love** (2:9). Verse 9 is itself a quotation from Isaiah 64:4 and 65:17. When Paul writes that "What no eye has seen, no ear has heard, and no human heart has conceived—God has prepared these things for those who love him," he does not mean to imply merely that heaven is an unimaginably great place. Many quote this verse and use it to mean that great things lie in store for believers. Though that is undoubtedly true, it would be grossly out of context for Paul to suddenly be talking about the glories of heaven. Instead, he is reiterating the natural and unregenerate person's incapacity to receive the things that God gives only to his people through the illumination of his Spirit. The emphasis is on the total inability of the *human heart* to conceive of God's work because it lacks divine wisdom. Only when God grants that wisdom can any human heart ever receive divine truth.

Living It Out

God's gift of his Spirit and, with him, the revelation of his truth, is the greatest demonstration of his love short of the cross itself. But the gift of the Spirit and of the cross are inextricably interwoven, because were it not for the Spirit revealing the meaning of the cross, everyone would think it foolish and no one would believe. Like the rulers of this age, even we would crucify the Lord of glory. But because of God's great love toward us, we see wisdom where the world sees only foolishness.

As the Word of God is preached, it meets with only one of these two conditions: either it is accompanied by the revealing power of the Holy Spirit or it is rejected by the sinner in his natural state of spiritual blindness. Though Paul has called all those who receive this message "mature" (2:6), he does not imply that this maturity can be attained through human intelligence or effort. In this immediate context, "mature" means all believers because they have divine wisdom. But that maturity has only one cause: God has revealed his message by his Spirit, so no one, no matter how accomplished in the study of the Bible, has reason for conceit or vanity. Whenever the Word is read or preached, believers should pray for the illumination of the Spirit to work powerfully through God's Word rather than relying on their own intellect for understanding.

The Effect of the Spirit

1 Corinthians 2:10–16

The Big Picture

Paul has just discussed what preaching accomplishes. The preaching of God's Word elicits two responses: either it is received by the hearer because of the Spirit's work, or it is rejected because the natural human state is a mind clouded by sin. The apostle continues this train of thought for the rest of chapter 2, revealing the effect and the necessity of the Holy Spirit's work in revealing truth.

Digging In

Building on his mention of the Spirit as the means of God's revelation, Paul informs his Corinthian audience of three ministries of the Holy Spirit. First, the Spirit *searches* all things, especially the deep things of God, because only the Spirit can relate to them (1 Cor. 2:10). This is the Spirit's **ministry of insight** (2:10b–11). The human spirit is not equipped to discern, comprehend, or appreciate spiritual things, any more than an ant can comprehend the global aviation system. An ant can only understand "ant things." Humans can know human things

25

because they have human experience, but when it comes to understanding divine things, only the Spirit can know spiritual things. If a human is ever to understand the message of the cross and all it implies, then he or she must have, not a greater intellect, but the Spirit of God himself bearing witness of the divine things.

Second, the Spirit *inhabits* every believer. This is his **ministry of indwelling** (2:12). At the moment of regeneration, as a sinner exercises repentance and faith, the Holy Spirit takes up residence within the newborn Christian. Notice the Trinitarian nature of such salvation. A believer received Jesus, the Son, by faith, because of the Father's plan effected by the Spirit through his convicting and regenerating work. When a person trusts Christ, she may not know much about theology. She may not read Greek. She has probably never heard of eschatology, much less understand it. But because she has the Spirit of God, she has the one thing needed to learn and apply spiritual things.

Finally, the third ministry of the Spirit is that he *teaches* in his **ministry of instruction** (2:13). Jesus promised this teacher to his disciples, so Paul says that "we also speak these things" to the "spiritual people," which in this context is another way of saying "those who are saved." The center of Paul's preaching is revealed in a vocabulary that only the Spirit can make meaningful. Words like *repentance, atonement, redemption, sanctification*, or *election* have no spiritual meaning to lost people. Though they may certainly understand their lexical significance, no unsaved heart leaps with joy that elicits a song of praise and a sense of gratitude. Only the Spirit teaches that rich significance and makes those words vital in the believer's life.

Just as those who aren't Egyptologists can't read hieroglyphics, a person apart from the Spirit cannot receive spiritual things. Paul means that the instrument an unbeliever relies on for interpreting what he sees is his own fallen, human spirit (2:14). He doesn't have the spiritual equipment to receive these spiritual things nor the spiritual wisdom to comprehend them. He has never learned the meaning of the words taught by the Spirit. Spiritual things seem only foolish because he is not equipped for spiritual discernment.

Paul contrasts the soulish person relying on his own spirit, with the spiritual person, the person in whom the Spirit of God lives. Because the saved person has God's Spirit, he has insight into matters that the natural person cannot. In fact, the Spirit of God influences the believer's entire world view, so that a person indwelled by the Spirit can make judgments about all things (2:15).

Consequently, the spiritual person is not subject to human judgment about truth. Paul is not suggesting that a believer is not subject to the legal requirements and judgments of society. He is speaking in the context of God's truth and his meaning is that one who knows and lives out God's truth is not concerned about the world's denial of the truth. In the same way, the believer's confidence does not lie in an innate ability to know truth, but in a complete dependence on "the mind of Christ" (2:16). As a believer learns Christ as revealed in the Bible and applied by the Holy Spirit, Christ becomes the lens through which the whole world comes into focus.

Living It Out

We never need *more* of the Spirit, because we have *all* of God's Spirit. We do, however, need to rely on the Spirit so that we understand more about what we got when we received Jesus. Jesus is not merely the elementary knowledge of the Christian faith. He is the sum total of that faith. No Christian knowledge ever goes beyond Jesus. We may learn more of Jesus, but we will never need anything *more than* Jesus. As the Spirit dwells in the believer, his presence constantly bears witness that the Christian may understand what God has freely provided in Christ. Having the Spirit of God influences what one thinks about life, marriage, finances, politics, fear, world events, and work. The perception and judgment of everything in life changes when one has the Spirit of God within, enabling the "spiritual" person to see clearly through the filter of God's wisdom.

The Holy Spirit's job is to help us understand all these great promises so that we can live holy lives. The Holy Spirit is not just an aid to our understanding, the Holy Spirit *is* our understanding. Without the Spirit of God, our preaching will only encounter the spirit of the world, which inevitably leads to rejection of the gospel.

But what man can know the mind of the Lord so that he can instruct God? Who can claim to know God's eternal purposes so that he can judge God's people? The answer to Paul's question in 1 Corinthians 2:16, a quote from Isaiah 40:13, is a resounding "No one!"

Though no one can instruct God, we can at least have his mind, the mind of Christ. Because we have the mind of Christ, we can receive and comprehend God's Word and God's will. Paul, however, is implying a deeper point. If we have the mind of Christ, why would we elevate men and develop factions behind personalities? The mind of Christ confers a spiritual capacity that we did not have before, but it also raises an ethical standard higher than we have ever known.

Baby Christians and Christian Babies

1 Corinthians 3:1–4

The Big Picture

Walk into any children's bookstore and you will find hundreds of brightly colored and creatively illustrated books that share a common purpose: to teach young children the alphabet. All parents who care about their children teach them how to recite and recognize the alphabet early in life. When a child enters the first grade, the teacher may ask, "Does your child know her ABCs?" No doubt conscientious parents feel some pride when they can triumphantly answer "Yes!"—even more so if the child is already a good reader. When that same child enters middle school, does the teacher ask if she knows her ABCs? Is that question asked of those who attend high school, college, or a doctoral program?

That question seems absurd at those levels, doesn't it? Nothing seems amiss when a first-grade teacher asks if a student knows the alphabet, but it would seem ridiculous to be asked multiple times later in life. By the time a student gets to college, teachers should be able to assume knowledge of the alphabet. No university should need to quiz applicants about the ABCs. A student would surely have to know the alphabet to get that far in the educational system.

Nothing is as inane as a doctoral student being asked about his mastery of the alphabet—except perhaps a Christian who can't master and apply the most basic truths and instructions of the faith. Unfortunately, churches often seem *filled* with Christians who have been in the faith for years, but somehow can't master the most basic truths. *That* is absurd.

As we move into the third chapter of Paul's epistle to the Corinthians, we detect a bit of impatience in the apostle. Even as he is indoctrinating and correcting them, his words convey a definite sense that he should not have to talk to them about such simple things. He laments that they "were not ready" for him to teach them what they should be learning because he must deal with basic things like "envy and strife," their worldliness and fleshliness.

Digging In

Is Paul saying in 1 Corinthians 2:1–3 that we ever get to outgrow the basics? Not at all. His words suggest, however, that because they are so basic, these truths should become a part of who we are and how we live our lives. We don't get *beyond* them, but we do grow deeper *in* them. We don't ever move *beyond* the alphabet, but all the wisdom in all the books in a library are simply different arrangements of the twenty-six letters taught to every English-speaking student. Though we ought to progress in our walk with Christ and in a deeper appreciation of his Word and his doctrine, we will never grow beyond the basic expectations like the need for unity, fellowship, glorifying God rather than man, and humility. In correction, Paul points out the spiritual immaturity that was obvious in the church at Corinth.

The Corinthian church had certainly lost its way and found itself operating with worldly wisdom. Paul wanted to correct them in a spiritual manner but could not because they were not using the Word of God as their reference point. All Christians sometimes get out of step with the Word, but those who are mature in their faith will accept the correction of the Word of God, whether it comes in their private devotion, a sermon they hear, or the loving rebuke of a friend. But when an individual or a church gets so far out of God's will that his Word no longer serves as their guide, then they first must be instructed to get back to the reference point. In this case, the Corinthians are falling horribly short of their high calling. Their actions are fleshly instead of spiritual, and by pointing this out, Paul intends that they should stop relying on the intuition of the flesh and, instead, live in the realm of the Spirit.

When Paul calls the Corinthian believers "babies in Christ," he is diagnosing their spiritual stagnation. If a child does not grow, he suffers from a desperately serious problem and needs medical attention. Likewise, the normal thing for a person who has received the gospel is to grow in Christ. When so many Christians fail to grow, the unnatural looks natural, and the abnormal looks normal. Instead of growing in Christ, the Corinthian church was a church embroiled in dispute, but hardly any of those arguments were worth having. In 1 Corinthians 3:3, Paul defines their fleshly outlook by pointing out their jealousy and quarreling over things that were not central to the gospel. They were unable to tolerate differences of personality and disposition. Their divisions were over petty differences and preferences. One telltale sign of immaturity among believers is the inability to distinguish between convictions that come from the Word of God and preferences that come from personal opinions.

The Corinthian calamity was filled with personality preoccupation (3:4). No doubt some of the members of the church followed Paul or Peter or Apollos just because they *liked* them. On the other hand, some based their loyalty on *performance*. Perhaps one of the leaders had done something that helped them, and so from then on, they felt allegiance to that person. Rather than simply showing appreciation to God for his use of men in the church, the Corinthians seemed to forget God and identify with the men themselves. That kind of behavior and allegiance belongs to the "mere human" realm rather than to the "spiritual" (3:4).

Living It Out

Are you a Christian who lives in the realm of the "merely human"? Have you become spiritually stagnant and intolerable by quarreling over things that don't matter? Do you find yourself embroiled in divisions in the church over personality preferences and differences? If so, you must not be content to remain in that condition but strive for holiness and obedience to Christ. Grow up!

"Worldly" (3:3) is Paul's way of speaking of the individual actions and outlook that reflect human nature more than divine character. He is rebuking them for their behavior. He is not providing a category of Christianity that one can live in as a second-class citizen and still go to heaven. On any given day a Christian may do many things relying on God's Spirit, but that same person may also do many things without him, too. To whatever degree a believer operates apart from dependence on God's wisdom and will, those things are fleshly or worldly. Living in that realm of flesh and repeatedly relying on worldly wisdom is a clear sign of spiritual immaturity and a reminder that we are not acting like what we are—partakers of the Spirit of God! Act like what you are! He has given you his Spirit, now live like you have him!

The Cure for Christian Babies

1 Corinthians 3:5–9

The Big Picture

When Paul saw spiritual immaturity in the church, he dared not let the Corinthians remain in that state. The seeds of destruction had already been planted and had to be rooted out by sound doctrine. As Paul reminds them that God alone deserves the glory even though he uses people, Paul advises them how to grow out of their immaturity and become the servants of God that the Lord called them to be and to see God as the one who gives increase to his vineyard, not the workers he sends to tend it.

Digging In

Central to Paul's questions, "What then is Apollos? What is Paul?" (1 Cor. 3:5) is a basic understanding that God's people are merely instruments in God's hands. Paul does not even ask, "*Who* is Apollos?" or "*Who* is Paul?" He uses the neuter rather than masculine form of the question to further indicate that people are only objects in the hand of a sovereign God who uses them as he wills. In fact, this is God's plan for growth in the church. He utilizes men and women to bring other men and women to the knowledge of the truth. Paul answers his own questions by indicating that God's envoys are nothing but servants. They are only the conduits who carried the Word to the Corinthians so that they could believe the gospel.

By picturing Apollos and himself as workers in God's field, Paul explains that, though they may have different jobs which entail different skills, they are nonetheless working for the same goal (3:8–9). Their common purpose is the production of fruit. Though they are inherently incapable of producing fruit themselves, they can each have a part in the process. Not one of their jobs is sufficient by itself. For the plant to produce, they each must do their part as God has assigned to them. Paul is reminding them that it does not matter *what* the job is, only that one *does* the job God has assigned. Then—and only then—do we become one, a single field, a distinct building (3:9). What a scandal that people in the Lord's churches don't get along better. Can you rejoice when someone else reaches the woman you have witnessed to and prayed for during the past five years? How do you feel when someone else's church reaches the people in your neighborhood? When believers appreciate that God gives different gifts to match the tasks to which he has assigned them, Christians should be the most compatible people in the world!

Paul is careful to point out that the laborers are not rewarded based on how much fruit is produced but based on their labor (3:8b). God sees and rewards all efforts made for his glory. The more one faithfully works in his field, the more reward one receives. Though God is gracious to reward workers for their labor rather than for fruit produced, productivity matters. The great news is that God is the one who "gives the growth" (3:7) We can have confidence that our labors will result in fruit because God himself is our co-laborer.

God may call someone to plant and someone else to harvest, but in God's mind one kind of labor is no more or less valuable than any other. Planting, harvesting, watering, and tending are all part of God's plan and will be rewarded. What a motivation to serve! Paul encourages the Corinthians that God has assigned each a part in his work, that he will reward according to one's labor, and he alone gives the increase and makes things grow. Nothing could liberate the Christian from pressure and compulsion, on the one hand, or provide motivation for any service more than that.

Paul makes an abrupt and important shift in pronouns in the second half of 1 Corinthians 3:9. He has been speaking primarily of himself and Apollos, instructing the Corinthians that they should not form factions around mere men who are, after all, only servants of God. He sums up that part of his argument with the simple sentence, "For we are God's coworkers." Then he suddenly changes to "*You* are God's field, God's building." Not only does Paul indicate that he and Apollos deserve no praise for whatever fruit God produced in Corinth, he also proposes that the Corinthians themselves are just a field or a building. A field cannot produce its own fruit and a building does not build itself. In other words, their chief duty is one of submission to God. As a field, they are tended; as a building, they are built. Through absolute submission to God—like a field or a building—God's will is realized and his purpose accomplished.

Living It Out

Understanding God's perspective on people provides a wonderful balance. On the one hand, this insight forbids jealousy, factionalism, and a haughty spirit. When we see others whom God uses in a more noticeable way than we seem to enjoy ourselves, we can still rejoice because we know that this is the Lord's doing. Rather than rally around personalities, even our own, the gospel itself becomes our rallying point. We realize that every person in the church has a role in God's plan.

On the other hand, this knowledge helps us understand that, so long as we are obedient to the Lord, we play an important role in the process. Being God's instrument precludes pride and forbids idleness. As a part of God's work, Christians do not have the right to engage in petty divisions or self-satisfaction.

Understanding that the production of this work and fruit isn't dependent on us keeps us from crumbling under the burden and strain of feeling that success might rely on our ability. Alternatively, if we thought that God would not reward our labors, we might throw up our hands in despair or grow complacent and quit. If we did not know that God gives the increase, we might be overwhelmed with discouragement that we do not see fruit as soon as we plant seed. Yet understanding each of these truths in their complimentary relationship keeps us enthused because our work will be rewarded, and God will use our labors to make things grow! We can count on it and anticipate his gracious recognition of all we have done!

When God's work is accomplished, though some have planted and others have watered, only God deserves any credit, any glory, or any allegiance, because only he made it grow. When the church has the sole desire to glorify him alone, differences of opinions and factions of personality vanish like the morning mist.

Day Ten

How to Build a Lasting Legacy

1 Corinthians 3:10–17

The Big Picture

After comparing the church to a field in the first part of chapter 3, Paul shifts the metaphor at the end of verse 9 and confronts the Corinthians with their personal responsibility in building the church. Certainly, a secondary meaning of the text is the care with which Christians should build their individual lives and the choices and decisions they should make, but Paul's *primary* meaning is the relationship of the believer to the church.

Digging In

Paul does not say that Jesus Christ is the *best* foundation; he writes that there is *no other* foundation. "For no one can lay any other foundation than what has been laid down" (1 Cor. 3:11a). The context is clearly addressing the local church, a particular faith community. Applying this to the way we build our individual lives certainly does no violence to the text. The meaning is as clearly personal as it is corporate. In the previous passage Paul addressed them as God's field, highlighting their corporate entity, but then he focuses on individuals. He shifts to talk about "each one's" work and that "no one" can lay any other foundation. He writes of the materials with which a single person may build. So, whether a community of believers or just one believer is in view, the truth remains: *you had better be certain what you are building on.* Jesus Christ is the only foundation.

The question remains, "How do we know him?" and it has only one satisfactory answer. Jesus, the incarnate Word, reveals himself through the Bible, the written Word. There must be no separation between the Jesus we worship and the Jesus of Scripture. To fashion a Jesus other than the one revealed in the Bible is to engage in idolatry and will always result in a God created in the image of man rather than vice versa. For this reason, Paul insists that there can be no other foundation (3:11).

No part of the building is more important than the foundation. Paul knew that he would not always be in Corinth to supervise the construction of the superstructure. He realized that others would have to build on the foundation he laid, but he called them to witness that he did not build the church on himself, or his rhetorical skill, or even on the apostles collectively. He laid the foundation of Christ alone. He will spend the rest of the letter to the Corinthians dealing with some of the inferior building that took place in the church, but first he calls them back to the basics of the person and work of Christ, the foundation.

Paul is quick to remind his readers that the foundation is not an end in itself. Not only must one be certain *on* what to build, But each one should be careful how he builds (3:10). Built on the right foundation and with the right materials, we can have tremendous confidence that our churches and lives will have lasting impact and do what God has purposed. Here, Paul reminds us that every aspect of our lives will be tried in time. The question is, "Will it last?" Whether we used inferior materials will become evident eventually. Paul warns that "the day will disclose it" (3:13).

The word *day* has a definite eschatological meaning. Throughout the Old Testament the prophets warned of the coming Day of the Lord,[5] and Paul uses that language here as he does in many other places.[6] He is referring to the future and final Day of Judgment when each person's work will be openly displayed. The books will be opened, and all will be judged according to their own works that have all been recorded (Rev. 20:12).

The only way to have confidence in the face of God's judgment is to use the best materials in every aspect of life. Who wants to go to heaven like the one Paul describes in 1 Corinthians 3:15? This man is indeed saved, but "only as through fire" (3:15). He lost everything except life itself, as though he makes it to heaven with the smell of smoke on him. Knowing that all will face such judgment, should make believers think constantly about how they are building and what materials they are using in their lives.

The temple that dominated Corinth both in size and its location in the heart of the city was the Temple of Apollo. Built in 540 BC, the temple was constructed of massive monolithic limestone columns, some of which still stand today. In a region known for its earthquakes and terrible destruction, the Temple of Apollo stood as a legacy of craftsmanship and design. When Paul wrote the Corinthians, the temple was already over six hundred years old!

In a city centered around a temple, Paul chooses exactly that metaphor to remind them that *they* are God's temple. In these verses, he seems to be speaking to them corporately again, addressing them collectively as the church. Now, centuries later, he is no less addressing us because we, too, are part of the number "in every place who call on the name of Jesus Christ our Lord" (1:2). We are not only choosing materials and doing the building, but we *are* the building. Because God's Spirit lives in us, we are the dwelling place of God, his temple. Everything we build—a life, a home, and primarily a church—will be tested by fire and proven by time. In the same way, God takes it seriously when anyone destroys his temple, his church (3:17). God's temple is *holy*. Now, Paul tells them, act like "what you are"!

Living It Out

Regardless of what particular gifts you may have, one thing is certain: you have enough grace to lay the foundation of Jesus Christ. The immediate application is undoubtedly to the church, but if we are wise master builders, then we will lay the same foundation in our homes and individual lives. Wisdom dictates that we build on Christ.

If we leave Jesus out, we lose *everything*. What made Paul a wise master builder was not his skill, but that he knew how to get the foundation right. When he planted the church at Corinth, he made the person and work of Christ central to his mission. We, too, can be wise builders by following his example. What are you building? Why are you doing what you are doing? Do you find yourself doing the right thing but often with the wrong motive? The only way our work will last is to build the right materials in the right way, and on the right foundation of Jesus Christ.

The Indispensable Reminder

1 Corinthians 3:18–23

The Big Picture

The world's thinking is completely the opposite of God's wisdom. Ever since Adam and Eve sinned in the garden, humanity has been plagued by "postlapsarian noetic effects." In other words, because of the fall, sin clouds the human mind and distorts its conclusions. Even worse, sin has bequeathed the mind an immense capacity for self-deception. Men and women the world over can convince themselves that obvious truths are false and patent falsehoods are truth. Foolishness seems wise and true wisdom seems foolish. The only way that anyone can be freed from this false "wisdom of this world" is to be illuminated by the Word of God applied by the Spirit of God who reveals the truth found in the Son of God. In these verses, Paul demonstrates to the Corinthians that their divisions and preoccupations with personalities are evidence that they are still thinking like the world and have failed to appreciate all that God has given them in Christ.

Paul had a secure sense of how he fit into God's plan and, therefore, the world in general. He had nothing to prove because he was living in God's calling and will, the only place contentment can be found. He deeply desired the Corinthians to enjoy the same sense of significance because their lack of it led to division and doctrinal aberration. So, before he teaches them about his role in their lives and in God's plan, he reminds them once again of their need to adopt God's perspective on men and wisdom. After Paul's lengthy discourse about God's "foolishness" and man's wisdom (1 Cor. 2:6–16), he used two metaphors in chapter 2, verse 9 to instruct the Corinthians about their own personal involvement and responsibility. As a field, they were passive, planted, watered, and tended by others, grown by God. As a building, though, they were active, choosing materials, building, and ultimately being tried by fire. In the last six verses of chapter 3, Paul returns to his initial instruction. First Corinthians 3:18–23 serve as the summary of his first section and begin a transition into his personal remarks about his relationship to the church at Corinth.

Digging In

The worst kind of deception is self-deception. Like a parent who wants to be certain that his children retain what they have heard, Paul repeats and summarizes the teaching of 1 Corinthians 1:18–2:16. They should accept God's standards rather than the standards of the age. Far better to be thought a fool by the world but to be initiated into God's wisdom (3:18) By repeating it here, Paul drives his admonition home in hopes they will recognize its importance and internalize it.

To root his teaching in the Old Testament, Paul references two texts that confirm the folly of human wisdom. "He catches the wise in their craftiness" from Job 5:13, asserts God's pattern of exposing the foolishness of those who think themselves wise. "The LORD knows that the reasonings of the wise are futile" refers to Psalm 94, specifically verse 11, a psalm which emphasizes how God thwarts the plans of the wise but blesses those who trust in him and follow his ways, his wisdom. Together these citations testify to the vanity of human reasoning apart from God's revelation of truth.

The logical conclusion of a comprehension of God's grace is that no one can boast in men whatsoever. John MacArthur points out that

Paul's teaching here presents (1) a proper view of ourselves (1 Cor. 3:18–20), (2) a proper view of others (3:21–22a), (3) the proper view of possessions (v. 22b), and 4) the proper view of our Possessor (3:23).[7] If each of the Corinthian believers would accept this teaching, the division in the church would erode and disappear altogether. Yet they persist in rallying around human leaders when each leader (such as Paul, Apollos or Cephas) is merely an instrument in the hand of God. There should be no envy in the church when everything—even their leaders, the world itself, life, death, the present, and the future—belong to them. They are like children in a room with thousands of toys fighting over a single wooden block. Why so much fuss and fighting when they own everything?

Here, Paul introduces a new element in his teaching beside what he wrote previously. He wants them to see their relationship to each other, to their leaders, and to God. "Everything is yours, and you belong to Christ . . ." (3:22b–23a). Then Paul adds a beautiful insight into the relationship between God the Father and God the Son: "and *Christ belongs to God*" (3:23). Paul's way of portraying the intimate relationship between the first two Persons of the godhead is unique, but he uses similar language later in chapter 11, verse 3 when he calls God the head of Christ. His meaning is one of relationship, not ownership. God does not *own* Christ, because they are One, but Christ relates to the Father in such a way that he possesses whatever belongs to God. In Paul's cosmology and in his instruction to the Corinthians, it's all about God. Everything belongs to him. The proper response, therefore, is to accept God's wisdom, but also his centrality in life.

Living It Out

God shares everything over which he exercises his lordship with his people. Wisdom, possessions, the world itself, all belong to him and he has graciously given it to us through Christ. If everything belongs to us, and we belong to Christ, we have no cause for envy, strife, factions, or glory. What can we want that we won't get? When our greatest desire is the glory of God, we will never be disappointed because God can get glory to himself from any circumstance in the life of his child.

Grace demands humility, and humility brings unity. Paul's phrasing that Christ belongs to God teaches us that even the godhead enjoy humility and unity, and so should Christians.

The Responsibilities of Stewardship

1 Corinthians 4:1–5

The Big Picture

If praising leaders is dangerous, Paul recognizes that a greater danger is to be the one put on the pedestal and praised. From the beginning of his rebuke of their loyalty to men, Paul has not demonstrated a hint of pride that some in Corinth esteemed him highly, nor of jealousy that others thought less of him than they thought of Peter or Apollos. So, if Corinthians are not to boast in these men who have ministered the Word to them, how should they think of them? More importantly to Paul, how should a leader respond to such adulation and acclaim? Chapter 4 is an integral unit with three subsections, each of them focusing on a respective quality of relationship that Paul enjoys with the Corinthians: Paul first explains the relationship as a manager, or steward (1 Cor. 4:1–5), then as an apostle (4:6–13), and finally as a father (4:14–21). As Paul fleshes out his responsibilities in each relationship, he teaches us about our own.

Digging In

If Paul was not to be praised nor placed at the head of some faction in the church, just how should the Corinthians regard and treat him? Some who admire him might treat him as a fourth-and-not-too-junior member of the Trinity. Others who feel an allegiance to Peter or to Apollos might disregard his teaching, even though it is of God, because they are jealous for their favorite leader. By applying his own illustrations to himself, Paul helps the Corinthians understand how to think of him, as well as other leaders. The key, Paul explains, is found in understanding the nature of his function as a servant of God.

The Christian Standard Bible translates 1 Corinthians 4:1, "A person should think of us in this way: as servants of Christ and managers of the mysteries of God." By employing these two words, "servant" (Gr. *huperetes*) and "manager" (Gr. *oikonomos*), Paul highlights two aspects of his ministry. His job is as a servant of Christ, to be sure, but specifically as a manager. As a servant of the Lord's, Paul's relationship is completely *vertical*. His focus must be on his relationship to his Master and whether he obediently performs the duties assigned to him. As a manager, he further suggests that the relationship entails maintaining a trust that has been committed to him by his master.

In the Greek household, wealthy families who had servants usually had one primary servant, the household manager, who was responsible for running the household. He (and it was always a he) handled the money, was responsible for decisions and purchases, instructed other slaves, and made sure that the household had necessary supplies.

Paul's relationship with the Corinthians and their treatment of him should be commensurate with his servanthood and stewardship. They should not regard him as a Christian superstar, worthy of adulation, nor as a *mere* slave, hardly worthy of notice. By calling himself a *steward*, several truths become evident. First, a steward's treatment by others is based on who his master is. Since the Corinthians honor Christ, they should treat Paul with respect, not because of any goodness or quality intrinsic to him, but because of who his master is. They may not approve of his rhetoric or value his appearance, but when he comes as a servant of Christ, his role demands an appropriate respect for his Master and his mission.

Second, the only basis of evaluating a manager is his faithfulness to care for what was entrusted to him. "In this regard, it is required that managers be found faithful" (4:2). Jesus illustrated this principle when he taught the parable of the talents in Matthew 25:14–29. When the master returned from his journey, he settled accounts with his stewards to see how well they had managed his money. Similarly, Paul defines his service to Christ as a management of the "secret things" or "mysteries" of God. God's redemptive plan of a crucified Christ is the core of that mystery that God has now revealed, and Paul will be evaluated solely on his care of that gospel.

Third, the only opinion of a steward that matters is the one held by his master. "It is of little importance to me that I should be judged by you or by any human court" (1 Cor. 4:3). Fellow servants simply aren't qualified to judge accurately, and even if they venture into passing judgment, their opinion is irrelevant. Paul states it similarly in Romans 14:4 when he writes, "Who are you to judge another's household servant? Before his own Lord he stands or falls."

And if fellow servants of Christ are in no position to judge, certainly unbelievers cannot judge Paul, either. They cannot even receive spiritual things and are following the wisdom of the world (1 Cor. 2:7–10). Paul will not submit himself and his gospel to any examination by any human authority. And if that be true, then Paul must take this truth a step further to its logical conclusion: *he is not even qualified to judge himself* (4:3b–4). Paul would bristle in indignation at some nebulous notion of one's conscience having the final moral authority in life. He knows that only God can judge his management of the gospel.

If the church should not expect leaders to please *them* rather than the Lord, it follows that leaders themselves should avoid the trap of trying to lead by pleasing everyone. If leaders comprehend the concept of stewardship, then they must focus on being a manager of God's resources and for God's approval alone. After all, even Jesus didn't please everyone. He testified, "The one who sent me is with me; he has not left me alone, for I always do what pleases *him*" (John 8:29 NIV).

Paul got it exactly correct when he said, "If I were still trying to please people, I would not be a servant of Christ" (Gal. 1:10). The minute we seek the approval and adulation of people, we abdicate our calling as a steward because we are more concerned about the open praise of men than the secret things of God.

A day is coming in which we will indeed be judged. The fourth truth Paul relates about his stewardship is that the manager won't be evaluated until his master examines the accounts. "It is the Lord who judges me. So don't judge anything prematurely, before the Lord comes, who will both bring to light what is hidden in darkness and reveal the intentions of the hearts. And then praise will come to each one from God" (1 Cor. 4:4b–5). Paul is not going to waste time worrying himself about why some factions in the church followed Apollos or Peter rather than him. By the same token, he will not spend so much time in introspective melancholy that he fails to fulfill his calling. Rather he is living in consideration of the coming examination when God will bring it all to light—including the "intentions of the hearts."

Living It Out

Paul's instruction to the church strikes an unfortunate contrast with so many contemporary churches. In some congregations the pastor assumes dictatorial power and lords it over God's flock, forgetting that he is primarily a servant. Other churches may so hamper and hamstring the pastor that he is not free to lead because they do not recognize that he is primarily God's manager, entrusted with the gospel.

We all pay lip service to the idea of pleasing God rather than men, but then we find ourselves wondering what others think. We hear criticism and our stomach knots up, even when we know that we are doing the right thing. Whenever we forget that faithfulness is a manager's first quality, we emotionally wipe ourselves out.

More churches need to practice the kind of esteem that Paul advocates. Church leaders must answer *first* to God because they are primarily *God's* servants and stewards of *his* mysteries. Church members owe their leaders esteem, but not worship. Leaders, on the other hand, must walk in humility, always guarding the gospel with which they have been entrusted. Many church problems would disappear overnight if pastors and members alike would truly understand the servanthood and stewardship that belong to the leader.

Day Thirteen

Living for the Smile of God

1 Corinthians 4:6–13

The Big Picture

Chapter 4 is one major unit with three subsections, each of which focuses on a respective quality of relationship that Paul enjoys. Yesterday's devotional highlighted Paul's relationships as a manager (1 Cor. 4:1–5). Today's section (4:6–13) highlights his relationship as an apostle. As a manager, Paul related on a vertical plane, servant to master. He had to answer "up," as it were. As an apostle, Paul relates both vertically—to *God*—*and* horizontally—to man. An apostle is sent *by* God *to* man. When Paul described himself as a manager, he was explaining a relationship into which no other human being could enter. He was accountable only to his Master. As an apostle, however, he is sent to involve and disciple others. People are inherent in the mission of an apostle.

Digging In

Beginning the section with the phrase "Now, brothers and sisters" (4:6), Paul gently moves to endear himself to his readers because a sharp

49

rebuke is coming in verse 8. Just as Jesus used parables to teach, Paul used images and metaphors (such as a field and of a building in 3:9). Though he did not name Apollos in the first five verses of the chapter, Apollos was surely in Paul's mind when he used the first-person plural "we" in verse 1. He wants no one to think that his teaching is in jealousy of or reaction against those who follow Apollos. He said all of these things so that they might learn not to take pride in one leader as opposed to another.

Verse 6 is notoriously difficult to understand in parts, especially what Paul means by "Nothing beyond what is written." In the first three chapters of the epistle, Paul introduced six Old Testament quotations with some form of the word "written" (1:19, 31; 2:9, 16; 3:19–20), so it seems likely that Paul is telling the Corinthians not to transgress the exhortations of Scripture ("what is *written*") and boast in mere humans.[8] The overall meaning is clear, however, because of the result clause at the end of verse 6. What Paul wants to see in the church is "that none of you will be arrogant, favoring one person over another."

Underlying the pride in the church was their failure to appreciate God's grace even in the giftedness of the ones they admired. But by putting his question in the second person, Paul's exhortation begins to sharpen and grow more pointed. "Who makes *you* so superior? What do *you* have that you didn't receive? If, in fact, *you* did receive it, why do *you* boast as if *you* hadn't received it?" (4:7, italics added). Paul is expressing one of the key concepts of Christian living. This is the secret both to humility and also being comfortable in one's own skin. True humility is not pretending you have no gifts. True humility is recognizing that *everything* one has is a gift.

Building on that very thought, Paul launches into his first volley of sarcasm in the epistle. More will come later, but his pen *drips* with derision, disdain, and mockery as he writes, "You are already full! You are already rich! You have begun to reign as kings without us—and I wish you did reign, so that we could also reign with you!" (4:8)

Their real problem is not the leaders around whom the several groups had rallied, but their own foolish pride and disdain for the grace of God. Little by little, Paul is peeling back layers of their pride and worldly view of life. They have lapsed into thinking like unbelievers.

Though he wants them to reign as kings, Paul knows that they cannot do so as long as they are trapped in worldly wisdom.

One of the ways Paul reminds his readers to "act like what you are" throughout his epistles is by going through a frequent pattern of exhortation, rebuke, and example. He exhorts them to the truth, then rebukes them for their departure from it, and then shows them an example of how to live the truth. First Corinthians 4 is a prime exhibit of this methodology. While the Corinthians think they reign as kings, the apostles are on assignment from God and they do not look like kings at all. Paul summarizes his very unkingly condition, as well as that of the other apostles, in four words: *spectacle*, *fools*, *weak*, and *dishonored* (4:9–10).

The Roman victory parade was a prized institution in the world of Paul's day. The conquering general would enter the city first, bringing his victorious army behind him, and then, last of all, leading in chains the captives taken in battle at the very end of the procession. Making their way through the streets and into the coliseum. The most prestigious captives would usually be slain "either at the hand of man or the teeth of wild beasts."[9] In contrast to the Corinthians who thought their wisdom and gifts made them reign as kings, Paul contends that God's favor may not necessarily take the royal route. His favor and power may be displayed in making his apostle a *spectacle*. How ironic that the apostles whom God placed first in the church (1 Cor. 12:28) are the ones whom God allowed to be spectacles to the world.

Paul returns to the language of chapters 1–2 when he remarks that the apostles have become *fools* (4:10), but in his appraisal of the Corinthians' wisdom, he is not paying them a compliment. Can anyone whom the world recognizes as great be following a crucified Christ? The third word Paul applies to himself and the other apostles is *weak*. One by one, he is rebuking all of the qualities the Corinthians admire. Paul was weak physically, to be sure, but he refers also to his spiritual weakness. He put no confidence in himself or in his talent. Ironically, God used those who knew their weakness rather than those who confided in their strength.

Finally, Paul describes himself as *dishonored*, and he enumerates the ways that he and his fellow apostles have suffered indignities for the cause of Christ. While the Corinthians were more attracted to the wealthy, well-dressed, and free from menial tasks, Paul's life was very different, because this is what has been required of his management of the mysteries of God. This is a briefer list of his hardships than he gives in 2 Corinthians 11:16–33, yet it makes the point. He has been deprived of normal sustenance, dressed in rags, beaten, and left utterly homeless. He has given up everything and suffered much for his Master. His humiliation extends even to his behavior. He has had to earn his living by hard labor; he has given up the right to curse those who curse him or to run from persecution. Summing it up, Paul's choice of a final descriptive word sums up his condition and strikes as a dagger at the pride of the Corinthians: he and the other apostles have become "the scum of the earth, like everyone's garbage" (1 Cor. 4:13).

Living It Out

Reading Paul's words we cannot help but be struck by how *opposite* the way of the world is from the way of the cross. The world says blessed are the mighty, but Jesus says blessed are the meek. The world honors the powerful, but Jesus honors the poor in spirit. The spirit of the age is to climb to the top and lord it over men, but the spirit of Christ is to become a servant of all. The world looks at the appearance, but God sees the heart.

But Paul and the apostles—like all those serious about their stewardship of the gospel—don't concern themselves with things that won't matter in eternity. What a bedraggled, unsightly lot they must have been with their threadbare clothes, calloused hands, and many scars. But every scar, every deprivation, every indignity and injustice they suffered for the sake of the gospel was noted and rewarded by the only one fit to pass judgment on them.

The Temptation to Please Everyone

1 Corinthians 4:14–21

The Big Picture

Paul has explained to the Corinthians why he cannot live to please them, either as a manager or as an apostle. He must please his Master, the one who sent him. Now in the third section of the chapter, he gets very personal and speaks to them as a father, a relationship that is horizontal, human to human, even though it is not a peer relationship. Like a good father, his goal cannot be to remain popular with his children. His responsibility demands that he admonish them, even when it puts an unpleasant strain on the relationship and intimacy.

Digging In

First Corinthians 4:14–15 remind the Corinthians of their *spiritual conception*. Paul reminds them that he is the one who "became your father in Christ Jesus through the gospel" (4:15). Paul does not claim responsibility for their salvation, as though it were of human will, but he can speak of himself as their spiritual father because of human agency. He planted the spiritual seed that resulted in the new birth. He is not being so stern with them because he wants them to feel bad, but because he admonishes them toward their calling in Christ.

Next, Paul reminds the Corinthians of their *spiritual maturation* (4:16–17). A father's job only begins at conception. He then must care for his children, ensuring their growth and instruction. A father's most effective method of teaching, of course, is by example. The simplest way to teach his beloved friends how to live for Christ is to simply say, "Imitate me" (4:16). Paul proceeds to explain "my ways in Christ Jesus, just as I teach everywhere in every church" (4:17). Openness and consistency are the hallmarks of reproducible ministry.

Knowing that the Corinthians had forgotten much in the intervening years, Paul promises to send Timothy, his most trusted protégée, to remind them of his way of life that he had taught them. A father cannot always be present in the lives of his children, but he is still responsible to make certain that they are cared for and instructed properly. In characteristic Pauline discipleship, this serves the double purpose of training Timothy as a teacher as well as training the Corinthians.

In all his dealings with the Corinthians, Paul is fatherly: he has begotten them, warns them, urges them, sets an example for them, and cares for their education. In the concluding verses of the chapter (4:18–21), he turns his attention to their *spiritual admonition* and, like a good father, sternly warns them of his impending discipline. If they do not change their patterns of belief and behavior, his next visit may be unpleasant for some of them. A paternal paraphrase of verse 21 might be rendered, "Don't make me come over there!"

Paul's fatherly leadership skills are noteworthy in these verses. While on the one hand he threatens them with an unpleasant encounter, he simultaneously isolates the arrogant troublemakers in the church by speaking of them in the third person as a subset of the church. "Certain ones have become arrogant as though I were not coming to you" is the literal rendering of verse 18. Then Paul continues: "But I will come to you soon, if the Lord wills, and I will find out not the talk, but the power of those who are arrogant. For the kingdom of God is not a matter of talk but of power" (4:19–20). By speaking to the church of the arrogant ones, he rebukes them, but he gives the rest of the church the opportunity to distance themselves, leaving Paul's opponents exposed and greatly weakened.

When challenging the "power" of the arrogant in Corinth and reminding them that the kingdom of God is not in word, but in power, Paul can only mean that he wants to know what these troublemakers can actually *do*. Can they build the church? Are they able to win the lost? The kingdom of God is not evidenced in one's life only by talk, but by the hand of God blessing and giving an increase. Are the arrogant members of the church able to bear the reproach that Paul has borne? Paul has stood before kings, suffered beatings, stonings, shipwreck, and abuse. The troublemakers speak boldly in Paul's absence, but he is confident that the power of God will expose them when he arrives.

As Paul concludes the section on divisions, he leaves them with a choice. They can have a stick or an olive branch. He will indeed come as a father, but whether he returns to Corinth in tenderness or in indignation is up to them and depends on their reaction to his letter. Either way, Paul determines to please God rather than man, and to do otherwise would ultimately harm the ones he tried to please.

Living It Out

Whether as a steward, an apostle, or a father, Paul's life is directed to the pleasure of God. Paul's simple admonition serves not only as a plan of action for the Corinthians, but also as a blueprint for godly leadership. Our goal should be to live for Christ in such a way that we can safely say, "Imitate me" to those who want to know how to live for Christ. Furthermore, Paul also knew the importance of training others to continue the cycle of teaching and raising up another generation of believers. Though he could not yet return to Corinth, he had already discipled a young Timothy who could stand in his stead and teach the truth.

Christian leaders take responsibility for the spiritual conception, maturation, and admonition of others. Being a spiritual parent often brings waves of joy and sorrow simultaneously, but no task is more rewarding. Whether as a steward who manages, a "spectacle" who suffers, or a parent who instructs, the Christ-follower does all for the glory of Christ.

The Compassion of Confrontation

1 Corinthians 5:1–13

The Big Picture

The first four chapters of the letter have focused on the divisions in the church at Corinth and their preoccupation with different leaders. The warning of 1 Corinthians 4:21 serves as a pivot from that topic as Paul turns his attention to another problem that has taken the church's focus off Christ and threatens to disrupt their unity. A member of the church has fallen into an immoral sexual relationship and, rather than being disturbed by his sin, the church has responded with arrogant pride at their own tolerance. First Corinthians 5, closely related to Matthew 18:15–20, provides the why and the how for loving church discipline. Paul has called them "saints," but when they refuse to rid the church of overt and unrepentant sin, they disregard the call to holiness.

Digging In

Paul had received the report that the Corinthian church was allowing sexual sin among the membership. This may not be surprising in a city like Corinth known for its debauchery and temple prostitutes. This sin, however, was of such a nature that even the pagans in Corinth would not excuse it. A man was having sex with his "father's wife," apparently his stepmother. Paul is aghast that the world's standards would be higher than the churches.

In verse 2, Paul reveals that he is as concerned with the church's lack of concern as he is the sin itself. Paul laments, "You are arrogant! Shouldn't you be filled with grief and remove from your congregation the one who did this?" (1 Cor. 5:2). They prided themselves, not in the fact that he was in sin, but in the fact that they could be *tolerant*, that they could overlook this as a private matter between him and God. They perhaps believed they were doing the right thing. Paul, however, suggests that they should be mourning as though someone had died. Their attitude had resulted in a desensitization to sin and its effects. In a spiritual sense, there had been a death, but they were yet to remove the unclean corpse from their midst.[10]

In 1 Corinthians 5:3–5 Paul instructs the church how to remove the brother who is in sin. For Paul, removal is the obvious result of living in sin while claiming to be a Christian. He repeats the command in some form in verses 2, 5, 7, and 13. Paul does not explicitly mention anything about forgiveness in chapter 5, probably because he had knowledge of the offending member's refusal to repent. We can safely conclude that this brother was unrepentant, that he was persisting in this sin, and that the opportunity for repentance had been refused. Closely echoing the words of Jesus as he encouraged church discipline in Matthew 18:20: "Where two or three are gathered together in my name, I am there among them," Paul assures the Corinthians that when they gather to deal with this sin, "I am with you in spirit, with the power of the Lord Jesus" (1 Cor. 5:4).

Removing a person from the church is no small thing. Paul calls it handing "that one over to Satan for the destruction of his flesh" (5:5), but the purpose is not merely removal, but restoration, "that his spirit may be saved in the day of the Lord." The apostle's hope is that the offending brother would feel the sting of sin's consequences and the community's absence and repent.

In verse 6 Paul turns his attention from the offender's sin to the church's attitude about it and questions them sharply. They do not see sin as serious and grievous as it in fact is. Not only is it harmful to the sinner, but also destructive to the church. Invoking Passover imagery in which no leaven is permitted, Paul reminds them that sin spreads through the entire church just like "a little leaven leavens the whole batch of dough." Since "Christ our Passover Lamb has been sacrificed," New Covenant believers perpetually celebrate the Passover. Leaven, or sin, is never welcome. We must rid the church of the "leaven of malice and evil" as we partake of "the unleavened bread of sincerity and truth" (5:8).

In 1 Corinthians 5:9–11 Paul explains that, for the Christian, separation is not from the sinners but from sin. He clarifies an earlier letter in which he told them "not to associate with sexually immoral people," explaining that he was referring to people who claimed to be believers, otherwise they would have to leave the world entirely. The Corinthian church apparently had everything backwards. They were separating from sinners outside of the church, thereby losing any impact, and tolerating sin within. Paul urges them not to separate from unbelievers who act like unbelievers, but when it comes to one who is called a brother, that requires separation from them.

When a professed brother will not repent, he should be removed from the fellowship and the members are not to even eat with such a person (5:11). Paul is either telling them to completely shun the removed offender or else he is referring to the meal that the church members share most commonly, their observance of the Lord's Supper.[11] Either meaning has huge implications and establishes boundaries of fellowship among Christians.

One thing is clear. Paul commands them to "Remove the evil person from among you" (v. 13). The church has no mandate to pass judgment on those outside of her membership because that is God's job (5:13), but the church has an unequivocal responsibility "judge those who are inside" their fellowship.

Living It Out

Sin is harmful, hurtful, painful, and deadly. Sin will be ruthless and merciless with the church, and the church should treat sin the same way. We must hate sin as God hates it, and we must love sinners as God loves them, but love requires honesty. The cruelest thing that we could ever do is see someone in sin and leave them there. Love demands that we confront them and call them to repentance. When we treat sin lightly, we will treat Christ's sacrifice lightly, as well. Sin is so awful and repugnant to God that it cost the life of Jesus. That is why Paul contrasts the church's arrogant and tolerant response to Christ's sacrificial death. The atonement demands holiness. Holiness cannot *earn* atonement; holiness *reflects* the atonement. The church of Jesus Christ must get rid of the leaven of sin because the Passover Lamb has been sacrificed!

The Right Way to Right Wrongs

1 Corinthians 6:1–11

The Big Picture

Following Paul's instruction on how to deal with the brother in sin (1 Corinthians 5), he expands his explanation of church authority and discipline to include the resolution of disputes within the church (6:1–11). His rebuke and instruction in these verses is not his typical orderly, logically framed argument, but rather an exclamatory, emotive reprimand that cycles through statement and restatement of the problem with solutions and theological underpinnings mixed in throughout.

Digging In

If Paul was disturbed by the church's tolerance of the adulterous affair, he discussed in chapter 5, he is no less scandalized by their practice of using Roman law courts to settle disputes between believers. Paul's provocation is evident by his use of the verb "dare" in verse 1.

The apostle is aghast at their assumption that justice can be found in the world more readily than in the church.

Paul rebuked the Corinthians for attempting to settle their differences before the ungodly rather than the saints. He leaves no doubt or wiggle room: Christians should not take their disputes before courts outside the church. This is consistent with his teaching in chapters 1–2 that only those who have received the Spirit of God have true wisdom.

Urging the Corinthians to take their matters before believers, Paul interjects an eschatological truth: "Or don't you know that the saints will judge the world? And if the world is judged by you, are you unworthy to judge the trivial cases?" (6:2). Paul's understanding throughout the epistles is a realized eschatology in which the blessings of the age to come have reached back into this age and are made real in the lives of believers today. His eschatology informs his ecclesiology, no doubt, because here he argues that the future destiny of the saved to judge the world should qualify them to judge petty cases within the church in this age. Compared to judging the world, almost anything would seem petty! Their recourse to civil courts of this world belied that they did not appreciate all that they have and are in Christ. They were not living in the present with a view of the richness of their future. Their "problems arose not just from bad ethics or social values but from bad theology."[12] Paul does not provide many details about the specific nature of this future judgment, but it resonates with Jesus' words to his disciples when they were arguing about which of them was the greatest and he reminded them "you will sit on thrones judging the twelve tribes of Israel" (Luke 22:24–30). Both Jesus and Paul argue from the greater to the lesser, reasoning that contemporary disputes between believers should be easily solved by those who will rule and reign with Christ. Paul adds that the saints will join the Christ in his judgment of the "world," the unrepentant. If the Corinthians will join Christ in future judgment, they should be able to join him in judgment in the trivial or mundane matters of the present age as well.

He restates his eschatological understanding by revealing in verse 3 that the saved will also judge the angels. If God is going to entrust them with the judgment of the angels, then certainly they should be able to handle the "matters of this life" (Gr. *biotika).* Since the

Corinthians already have the Spirit of God, they already have access to divine wisdom.

The overall meaning of 1 Corinthians 6:4–6 is that the Corinthians have settled for an inferior justice because they opted to adjudicate their matters before unbelievers who lack God's Spirit. They have not allowed the incursion of the wisdom of God into their everyday affairs. Paul's pen drips with sarcasm as he asks, "Can it be that there is not one wise person among you who is able to arbitrate between fellow believers?" His astonishment is understandable, because these are the same people who have so valued "wisdom" that they formed factions around their favorite leader. These are the same people who disregarded Paul because he didn't use flowery language and rhetorical wizardry when he spoke. For all their admiration of wisdom, their use of secular civil courts was an admission that no one among them could exercise good judgment.

For Paul, consistency of thought and life was paramount. A glaring inconsistency like this in the lives of the Corinthians struck the apostle as scandalous and shameful on two counts. First, no brother should be going to law with another brother in the first place because God has given believers his wisdom. Christians should be able to settle differences because they have God's Spirit. Second, the disagreements of Christians should not be aired before unbelievers because of testimony. Paul believes this so strongly that he lays down the principle that being wronged and cheated is preferable to going to secular courts, which is, in itself, "already a defeat for you" (6:7).

Verse 9 begins one of Paul's "vice lists" (cf. Gal. 5:19–21; Col. 3:5; Rom. 1:26–27; 1 Tim. 1:9–10), in which he bluntly spells out characteristic sins that exclude people from the kingdom of God because they are inconsistent with the Christian life and the character of Jesus. These verses serve as a transitional passage into the discussion of immorality that follows in the remainder of the passage. The apostle's main idea serves as a warning and a reminder to the Corinthian believers that they must not sell themselves short. By seeking gratification and satisfaction in this life, they lose sight of the joy of the kingdom that God has designed for them.

The blood of Jesus Christ is greater than *any* sin. Neither homosexuality nor any other sin presents a challenge to the grace or love of God.

What began as an instruction about settling their differences concludes with an appeal to the great truth that unites them in heart and in purpose. How can those who have experienced the deliverance of redemption become so wrapped up in petty squabbles? How can the redeemed live in the sin from which Christ delivered them? Both situations demand a reorientation to live in view of the joy of life with Christ.

With joy in his heart, Paul reminds the Corinthians that many of them were in that very condition. "And some of you used to be like this. But you were washed, you were sanctified, you were justified in the name of the Lord Jesus Christ and by the Spirit of our God" (1 Cor. 6:11). Paul connects his appeal to them with the reminder of God's grace and mercy. This verse should drive a sinner to his knees in repentance with the knowledge that he can be saved, and it should drive a child of God to his knees, too, in gratitude for what God has done. It requires no more of the blood of Christ to save an adulterer, a homosexual, a greedy person, a drunkard, a slanderer, or a swindler. To transgress in one point is to be guilty of breaking all the law (James 2:10). Whatever the sin, the blood of Christ can wash, sanctify, and justify the sinner!

Living It Out

Seeds of discord and discontent lie hidden even in the best churches and in the most Spirit-filled individuals. Any church in the world will find legitimate problems, disagreements, and misunderstandings in its members, but that church cannot expect to find a true solution to the problem in a civil court. Christians should be able to resolve disputes with Christians, particularly by adopting the attitude that it would be better to be wronged than to misrepresent Christ to the world.

As important as the immediate topic of lawsuits and sins may be, we need to pull back from the particular issues to think carefully about Paul's reasoning, because it applies to every aspect of the Christian life. If we have the Holy Spirit, then we have all we need to (1) settle disputes with other believers and (2) abandon the sins of our past. Nothing causes greater harm to the gospel than the people who claim to believe it when they fail to live it out. God has given us his wisdom and his grace so that, whatever problems and temptations come, we are equipped to resolve it in a way that brings glory to Jesus.

Day Seventeen

Getting a Grip on Our Sexuality

1 Corinthians 6:12–20

The Big Picture

Though the world has grown more creative and found novel ways to indulge lust, a selfish misappropriation and unbalanced treatment of sex is as old as the record of Genesis. Corinth was especially known for its sensuality, a city accustomed to prostitution, sailors at port, adultery, divorce, and typical Greek sexual practices such as homosexuality and pederasty. When Paul arrived at Corinth and preached the gospel, his audience was one that was thoroughly immersed in a culture of sensuality and lust.

Since Paul's departure from Corinth, some members in the church had misapplied aspects of his teaching to misconstrue a theological excuse for their indulgence in sin, claiming that, since they were not under the law, "Everything is permissible" (1 Cor. 6:12). Once again, Paul explains that they have a theological problem as well as an ethical problem.

Digging In

Throughout 1 Corinthians, Paul quotes pithy slogans, probably reported to him by members of Chloe's household (1:11), that were apparently popular in the church. Paul knew that they reflected a popular, though aberrant, theology believed in the church. Usually the maxim is a half-truth with just enough basis in Paul's teaching to seem plausible, and just enough error to steer someone into heresy or sin.

These verses in the second half of chapter 6 have several of them, the first of which is "Everything is permissible for me" (6:12). The Christian Standard Bible puts quotes around the phrase to denote that Paul is quoting them rather than generating the statement himself. Both times he quotes the adage he immediately responds with a "yes, but . . ." qualification. Even if something is *permissible*, it isn't necessarily *beneficial*, and even permissible actions should not "master" the believer.

Paul's response provides believers with an important filter when contemplating an action. *Freedom requires responsibility.* Even if the action is not necessarily wrong, is it truly "beneficial"? If it does not aid one's walk with Christ, if it does not display love for brothers and sisters, if it does not edify others or help reach the lost, then it should be abandoned. Some actions might be good and right in themselves, but if they are overindulged, then life grows unbalanced and even the good thing becomes master rather than servant. Ironically, many of the very things that Christians do in the name of freedom result in their bondage.

First Corinthians 6:13 has another slogan, "Food is for the stomach and the stomach for food," indicating the close connection between food and sex in the ancient world. The Corinthians were suggesting that all these pleasures were from God and, therefore, available without restriction to believers. Since God will one day destroy everything physical, they reasoned, nothing done in the body will matter in the age to come. If only the spiritual realm matters, whatever a believer does with the body is permissible.

Paul responds to their flimsy logic by countering that they cannot possibly separate the spiritual life from their bodies. The body is "for the Lord," not for sexual immorality (6:13), and the Lord is "for the body" as well. Christians are "for the Lord" by creation and obedience, but the Lord is "for the body" by promising the resurrection. Paul explains further in 6:14 that, contrary to what the Corinthians were teaching, the body does not go out of existence at death but awaits resurrection and glorification in the resurrection just as Jesus' body did. Just as in his instruction about lawsuits (6:2–3), Paul roots Christian behavior in an eschatological reality.

If the church at Corinth is a body of Christ (12:27), then each person in the church is a member of Christ's body (6:15). Whatever they do to their bodies, therefore, they do to Christ. They cannot separate their physical activities from their spiritual lives, much less from their vital union with Christ. *Sexuality affects spirituality!* The thought of uniting members of Christ with a harlot fills Paul with such horror that he responds forcefully, "Absolutely not!"

To complete the picture, Paul draws the unmistakable parallel between human sexual relations and spiritual intimacy. The act of marriage, of loving intercourse between a husband and wife, is the human relationship that most closely resembles intimacy with God. With God's design for intimacy so clearly revealed on both levels, believers must never be satisfied for less than God's intention either in marriage or union with Christ. The two reflect one another.

Paul's response to sin is never a simple, "Stop doing that!" He always moves the focus from the sin to the Lord. He follows, "Don't unite with a prostitute," with, "But anyone joined to the Lord is one spirit with him" (6:17). In other words, spiritual intimacy is the only way to overcome illicit sexuality. The Christian cannot divorce sexuality from spirituality but must seek spiritual union with Christ *first.*

Sexual purity matters because *immorality brings mortality.* A sexual sin is a sin against one's own body and in a category different from all other sins (6:18). If a man steals, he can repay it, but where does one go to get one's virginity restored? If a man kills, he sins against another human being; but if a man commits a sexual sin, he sins against a sexual partner *and* his own body. If married, he also sins against his wife and family. No other sin embarrasses and hurts quite as deeply. No other sin is so wrapped up in a matrix of emotions. No other sin so crushes the spirit of the innocent ones sinned against.

As a final rebuke to the false thinking of the Corinthians, the apostle finally explains why they cannot possibly excuse their sin by discounting the spiritual significance of their bodies. Using the phrase, "Don't you know . . ." for the eighth time in the letter, he rhetorically expresses his incredulity at their ignorance of the most basic Christian principles. Reminding them of the truth he already expressed in 1 Corinthians 3:16–17, Paul reiterates their role as the temple of the Holy Spirit (6:19). In chapter 3, he spoke of the church's role as the temple, but here, he focuses on the individual. Since the Holy Spirit resides in them, they are a sanctuary, a temple of the living God.

Going beyond the image of a temple to that of a slave Paul insists that they are bought at a price and do not have the right of self-determination. What slave tells his master what he is going to do? In this case, being a slave to Christ is totally unlike any slavery the world has ever known. He is the perfectly kind, loving Master who always does what is best for his servants, but since he is perfectly good, he is also perfectly right when he commands his servant. As a temple, they are to be holy. As a slave they are to be faithful. *Submission brings fidelity.* Submission as the residence of God leads to faithfulness as the servant of God.

Living It Out

Freedom in Christ is key to understanding Paul's teaching about salvation and the grace of God, but two warnings should be attached. First, we dare not let a fear of overreaction and twisting of this teaching keep us from teaching it. On the other hand, we dare not preach *only* grace without a message of love and obedience. Then we fall into a sugary spirituality devoid of any emphasis on developing Christlike character. Like Paul, we may have to frequently return to the subject and explain that grace does not imply licentiousness. Every road has two ditches and our enemy really does not care which one we fall into. Liberals don't see God's holiness; legalists don't see God's heart. May God give us the grace to live for him, body *and* spirit, in freedom *and* responsibility.

Day Eighteen

Honoring God in Marriage or Singleness

1 Corinthians 7:1–9

The Big Picture

After correcting the libertine notions of sexuality in 1 Corinthians 6:12–20, Paul then moves to confront the opposite problem. Some members claimed that celibacy, even within marriage, was the best way to live. The church at Corinth had completely reversed God's design! Our Creator's intention and instruction for sexuality and marriage should be the standard for everyone, but especially for believers who trust him. He made us sexual beings and then instructed us in how to express that very intimate part of our lives in a way that is most satisfying to us and most glorifying to him. Marital sex can be one of the greatest sources of joy and pleasure or it can be a fount of filth and pain, depending on whether one submits to God's teaching and learns how to live selflessly as God directs. Similarly, singleness submitted to Christ can be a liberating means to a life of Christian service and devotion.

Digging In

This is the first time that Paul refers explicitly to a letter that he had received from Corinth. The phrase translated "Now about" in 7:1 also occurs to introduce a passage in 8:1, 12:1, 16:1, and 16:12, and in each case seems to reflect a particular question they had asked the apostle. In this case the authors of the letter had written, "It is good for a man not to have sexual relations with a woman" (7:1), as though avoiding sex somehow made them holier. Using their slogan as a springboard, Paul instructs the church on marriage, singleness, divorce, and contentment throughout chapter 7. He does not approach these subjects in a systematic way dealing with them one subject at a time. Instead, he states and restates, questions and answers, shifting easily between subjects but always returning to the central concept of contentment.

Paul's fluid movement between his anchor points highlights the connectedness of life. Though the experience of a married person may be very different from that of a single person, as believers their foundation and goal are the same. The foundational truths are . . . that Paul teaches in chapter 7 is the lordship of Christ in every area of life, and God's glory as the greatest goal. These twin truths form the core of the Christian worldview and life decisions.

Paul begins this section by speaking first to the married members of the church at Corinth. His tone changes from the abrupt and even stern tone of chapters 5 and 6 to a much warmer, pastoral quality as he shows sensitivity to the difficult and intimate areas of life. He quotes their slogan, "It is good for a man not to use a woman for sex" (author's paraphrase), and then responds in blunt detail. He has already dealt in part with the "libertines," now he must correct the "ascetics," who advocate singleness as an inherently godlier lifestyle and even propose that married couples should be celibate, too.

The apostle's response is direct and unambiguous: sex is exclusively between a husband and wife (7:2), is a "duty" rather than an option in marriage (6:16), helps avoid sexual sin (7:2), and is an act of mutual submission between husband and wife (7:4). Each partner must help the other avoid sexual temptation by being sexually available. Insofar as married persons fail to satisfy the legitimate and reasonable sexual needs of a spouse, they are out of the will of God.

Paul's directive is both liberating and limiting. Each partner has a freedom with the body of the other, but a limitation is placed on his or her own. This strikes the balance that often gets left out of an age and a culture in which everyone insists on their own rights. Paul knows very little of rights, because he sees everything through the lens of undeserved grace. Ideally, married people who view each other through that lens will have the glory of God as the goal and avoid the extremes of being demanding or depriving of the other.

First Corinthians 7:5 clarifies Paul's instruction: married couples are to enjoy the sex act regularly. "Do not deprive one another . . ." does not mean that no married person should ever lovingly and politely defer because of exhaustion or tension, etc. Deferment is not deprivation. The habitual and recurring enjoyment of married sex should only be interrupted, Paul says, when a couple agrees to a special season of prayer (7:5). Neither partner has the right to be demanding and forceful because *both* partners have yielded control of their body to the other (7:4). One cannot demand something of the other and simultaneously claim to have yielded his or her own body. This mutual submission requires that both husband and wife seek the Lord and pursue holiness *together*. That is what "one flesh" requires.

Knowing that Satan takes such advantage of sexual appetites, Paul remarks that his one exception for sexual frequency is not a command but a concession (7:6). In other words, Paul is certainly not commanding that married couples abstain from sex during seasons of prayer, but he is saying that is the *only* reason that they should ever go through a period of abstinence.

Paul viewed both marriage and singleness as a gift from a gracious God (7:7). Recognizing that God has an individual plan for each of his children, Paul acknowledges that each one must live according to the gifts God has given. Some are given the desire to marry, while others are given the ability to remain single. Not all singles lose their desire for marital companionship, yet God gives them the grace to find fulfillment in their relationship with Christ.

Paul only briefly addresses singleness in chapter 7, verses 8–9, deferring much of his instruction to later in the chapter. He includes singles and widows here, however, because the instruction for them has the same goal as that of married couples: to honor the Lord with obedience in whatever life circumstance you have. Paul affirms the value of singleness. By explaining the significance of each mode of living, Paul implies that holiness does not depend on whether one is married or not. Though he offers some strategies that help avoid temptation and sin, he nonetheless avers that both married and single people can honor the Lord, even in the most intimate area of their lives.

Paul appreciated the single life and remained committed to it. For him, remaining single was practical. Later in the epistle he will argue for the *right* to marry but explain that he does not because of practical reasons. Though Paul commends the single lifestyle to others, his reasons were not selfish. He cherished his singleness because it put him completely at the Lord's disposal. But Paul also acknowledged that celibacy is not for everyone. Though his experience of singleness was positive, he realized that the basic plan for God's children is marriage. He counsels those who are single that if they stay that way, they should celebrate their singleness and devote themselves to the Lord, but if they have a strong sexual desire and fear that they will succumb to temptation, they should marry.

Living It Out

Behind all of Paul's counsel lies the implication that we must be completely honest with ourselves about ourselves. The Christian has no room for self-delusion, and the only way we can truly know ourselves is through intimacy with God. As we spend time in his Word, we get a true picture of ourselves and of how we conform to the image of Christ.

Marriage and singleness both require a total dependence on the Lord. In marriage we must draw on his wisdom and strength to live with another person, frequently surrendering our own rights and desires, often struggling to find that middle ground between competing views and desires. Those who remain single must rely on the Lord for the strength to remain chaste and to find contentment in Christ. Whether married or single, we all must learn the great truth that we exist for his glory and pleasure, and not for our own.

Honoring God– Anyway

1 Corinthians 7:10–24

The Big Picture

These verses mention a lot of controversial things: divorce, remarriage, circumcision, slavery, and living in difficult situations. Despite so many topics, Paul really has only one subject: serving Christ whatever your circumstances may be. While making that point, he provides the Corinthians with some very direct teaching about marriage, divorce, and remarriage.

To keep the passage in context, we need to remind ourselves of Paul's transition from his instruction on sexual purity in chapter 6 to his pastoral advice on marriage and singleness in chapter 7. The hinge on which both doors swing is his declaration that we are not our own because we have been bought with a price, the blood of Christ. Based on that, Paul demands that we should honor God with our bodies (1 Cor. 6:19–20). Everything that follows is a fleshing out of what that looks like practically. In the first part of chapter 7, he instructed married people to honor God by giving themselves freely to their mates (7:1–7). Next he directed the unmarried and the widows to honor God by their chastity, but if they burned with passion, they could honor God by getting married. But what about those who are in a *bad* marriage? How can they please the Lord? Paul's instruction is simple and forthright: if possible, *stay married.*

Digging In

In 1 Corinthians 7:10 he addresses the wife and in 7:11 the husband, and to each he gives the same command: don't divorce. The witness of Scripture about this principle is strong. From the garden of Eden when God united Adam and Eve, his standard has always been one man for one woman for life. Man deviated from God's plan many times, whether through polygamy or divorce, but God has always been clear about his intent. "This is why a man leaves his father and mother and bonds with his wife, and they become one flesh" (Gen. 2:24).

Because God"s Word is so clear about the permanence of marriage, Paul adds that this command is from the Lord, and is nothing new from him ("not I, but the Lord"—1 Cor. 7:10). The Corinthian church may have witnessed a rash of divorce proceedings initiated by the wives because Paul aims his remarks to the women first. After counseling them not to divorce, he further forbids them to remarry if they leave: "she must remain unmarried or be reconciled to her husband" (7:11). Adding, "and a husband is not to divorce his wife," Paul applies the same standards to the men.

Paul is just echoing and applying Jesus' teaching on marriage. During his ministry, the Lord, also, set such a high standard for the marriage covenant (cf. Matt. 5:31–32; 19:1–12) that Jesus' disciples responded that, "it's better not to marry." Reading the words of Paul in 1 Corinthians 7:10–17, we are left feeling much like the disciples after they heard Jesus' teaching on marriage and divorce. *Who can do this?* Though Jesus and Paul both give narrow exceptions to this instruction, the clear meaning of the text is that Christian people should value marriage and strive to honor one another and the Lord by keeping the marriage covenant.

What does Paul mean in verse 12 when he says that he is saying this and "not the Lord"? Paul is contrasting this with what has gone before in verse 10 because his instruction on marriage and divorce thus far has been found elsewhere in the Old Testament and in the teaching of Jesus. Jesus, for instance, taught that adultery makes divorce permissible, though not desirable (Matt. 5:31–32). Now Paul presents a second exception clause, a teaching on divorce that is not found previously in Scripture. In 1 Corinthians 7:12–14, Paul instructs that if a believer is married to an unbeliever, they should stay in the marriage. No one should ever use his or her faith as a reason for divorce as though God desired the dissolution of the marriage. If the unbeliever is willing to stay in the marriage, the believer cannot leave just because he or she struggles to follow Christ with a spouse who is lost.

If, however, the unbelieving mate leaves, no longer willing to be married to a Christian, then Paul counsels them to let the lost spouse go (v. 15). Paul's words, "A brother or a sister is not bound in such cases" can only mean that the believer is free to remarry if he or she is deserted by an unbelieving spouse. If a widow is not bound (Rom. 7:1–3), but free to remarry, then saying that the victim of desertion is not bound must certainly indicate the same thing.

Though not explicitly stated in the text, Paul is speaking to recent converts (as the Corinthian church was just a few years old), so the freedom to remarry would only apply to those who were unbelievers when they married but have accepted Christ since. He provides no exception for a believer who married outside of the will of God by wedding an unbeliever (see 2 Cor. 6:14–18).

The Corinthians seemed to be looking for reasons to abandon unbelieving spouses, perhaps claiming that a believer was defiled by marriage to one who refused to trust Christ. In 1 Corinthians 7:14 Paul asserts that the opposite is true. The unbelieving spouse and children are set apart or "made holy" because of their attachment to a believer. Paul is probably echoing Jewish concepts of betrothal and marriage.[13] They need not worry that they are defiled by their family members. Furthermore, by staying, they can continue to have influence and to be a gospel presence (7:16). Peter says much the same thing in 1 Peter 3:1–2.

Paul makes it clear in 1 Corinthians 7:17–24 that these principles are not for married people; they are for *Christian* people. He is dealing with a basic human tendency, the predisposition to see our situation as tougher than others, to hold ourselves as above the rules, and to think our circumstances are the *real* problem in our lives. People leave marriages, jobs, and churches all the time, only to discover that their problem was not geographical. There may be legitimate reasons to leave any or all those situations, but a Christian's default position should be to seek a way to serve God faithfully, even in difficult circumstances.

By insisting that the church should "let each one live his life in the situation the Lord assigned when God called him" (7:17), Paul asserts God's sovereignty and strategic purpose in saving people. That circumstance may be marriage, Judaism, paganism, slavery, or freedom (7:17–23). If God, in his providence, should change that circumstance, then they should use that, too.

Launching from his instructions to slaves, Paul comes back to the hinge on which his entire treatment of marriage, divorce, remarriage, and circumstances hangs: "You were bought at a price" (7:23). Knowing that they belong to the Lord should free the Corinthians from the slog of their circumstances. Whatever they may do, and whatever their status, they are not slaves of other people, but they have been bought by the Lord. Even better, the Lord bought them to free them. Knowing this infuses the drudgery and dreariness of life with a beauty and a devotion that God sees and honors.

Living It Out

The lordship of Christ places demands on us that the rest of the world cannot understand. Serving a Savior who *endured* the cross gives us a motive and an ability to endure tough situations because it honors God and reflects his character.

When we struggle with our circumstances and take our eyes off Christ, we may begin to believe the lie, that obedience depends on circumstance. "If only I were somewhere else" or "If only I had a different job" or "church" or "spouse." The moment that we entertain that notion and begin to blame our circumstances for our disobedience, the awful lie begins to gnaw at our peace and our submission to the will of God. We stop seeking God and start seeking our own way out.

We must not deny that many people do indeed face circumstances such as abuse, adultery, or abandonment that warrant or necessitate a change. It's not always wrong to change our circumstances, but we must ask and answer an important question: which do we prize more, happiness or holiness? You cannot be "happy" in the normal sense of the word in a marriage to a spouse with Alzheimer's, but you can be holy. Your life on this earth may take the courage of a thousand heroes just to get up and face each day, but you must settle the issue of whether life is to be lived for you or for the Lord who bought you. You may not enjoy the kind words of an encouraging spouse as often as you might want, but you can know the affirming smile of God who is pleased by your faithfulness. You may not have the solace of sexual intimacy, but you can have the comfort of the Holy Spirit. You may never hear the appreciation of a grateful wife, but you can hear, "Well, done, good and faithful servant" (Matt. 25:23).

Day Twenty

Godly Advice for Singles (and everyone else!)

1 Corinthians 7:25–35

The Big Picture

As Paul takes the Corinthians through what it means that "you were bought at a price," he focuses especially on the matters of sexuality, marriage, divorce, and remarriage. This is because of their pagan setting in Corinth, but also because these issues had plagued the church. He issues a challenge and an exhortation for singles in the church as well, because they share many of the same temptations, and also some that are unique to their singleness. Seeing beyond the temporal loneliness that they may feel, he calls them to the tremendous impact they can have on the world for the sake of the kingdom.

Though much of this text is addressed directly to singles, in a style characteristic of this entire section, Paul also turns his attention to other subgroups and provides instruction that serves as a unifying principle for them all. In this text, Paul's proposition is that every believer should honor God by making him the priority.

Digging In

When Paul addresses "virgins" in 1 Corinthians 7:25, he means people of both genders of marriageable age who have remained single. He gives them pastoral advice "as one who by the Lord's mercy is faithful" (7:25). Unlike much of his instruction on marriage, he cannot quote anything directly from the teaching of Jesus or from the Old Testament, but he uses his sanctified common sense, his vast experience, and the Spirit of God in his apostolic role (v. 40) to reiterate his counsel for them to "remain as he is" (v. 26), the theme he began in the previous section of chapter 7.

Paul has already advocated singleness as a healthy lifestyle for a Christian. What distinguishes this teaching is that he adds two reasons for remaining single. The first is "because of the present distress" (7:26). What is this distress or exigency to which Paul refers? The most likely meaning of these verses is that Paul's reference is eschatological, a forward look to the consummation of the age at the return of Christ. The apostles knew and taught that Jesus had already fulfilled the mission of his sinless life and ministry, his sacrificial death and victorious resurrection and ascension to the right hand of God. The next item on God's agenda is the return of Christ.

Knowing that Christ will come back soon and that his coming may be preceded by and accompanied with trials and tribulations, Christians should feel a sense of urgency and expectation that elevates our interest above the things of this world. In view of this urgency, this impending crisis, Paul counsels the unmarried to stay that way.

He reminds the Corinthian believers that his advocacy of celibacy does not apply to those already married. "Are you bound to a wife? Do not seek to be released" (7:27). They have no right to claim eschatological reasons for abandoning a spouse. Paul indicates that once a Christian man or a woman gets married, the natural and right thing is to meet the responsibilities incumbent on them because of their commitment, echoing Ecclesiastes 5:5, "It is better not to vow than to make a vow and not fulfill it."

But his advice to the unmarried is unmistakable: "Are you unmarried? Do not look for a wife" (7:27b). This is good advice for *any* single man or woman, not only those who have the gift of celibacy. A mate is not the solution to all problems or temptation. People who cannot control themselves sexually outside of marriage will probably struggle even when married.

Marriage and singleness are both gifts from God and neither one is inherently more sanctified than the other. God gives both to individuals as he will. But whether married or single, Christians must not lose the sense of urgency that the imminent return of Christ demands. Looking for the return of Christ should govern the lives of married and single Christians alike.

While Paul does not suggest that the Corinthians should neglect the duties of life or lose the balance necessary to live on this earth, he is reminding them that this world is not home. Because their redemption has been paid and "the time is limited" (7:29), their perspective is changed forever. Though they still live here, they live in anticipation of the appearance of Christ and a move to a new home. Because the time is so short, the normal human activities like weddings, funerals, parties, commerce, and the possession of things don't mean as much. In 7:29–31, Paul uses a rhetoric of hyperbole, similar to that used by Jesus when he said, "If anyone comes to me and does not hate his own father and mother, wife and children, brothers and sisters—yes, and even his own life—he cannot be my disciple" (Luke 14:26). After arguing so strongly about marital responsibilities, it would hardly make sense for Paul to encourage married people to abandon their partners. He is, however, insisting that their allegiance to Jesus comes first. Marriage and families are important, but those relationships belong to this age. Our relationship to Christ is eternal. Paul is pointing his readers to the *eschaton*, the age to come. The awareness of the relatively short time until Jesus returns, and the temporary nature of all things demand that they place God above everything.

In 1 Corinthians 7:32–35, Paul further extols the benefits of serving Christ as a single person. A married person necessarily weighs decisions for how they affect spouses and children. Paul clearly understands that not everyone has the gift of singleness, but those who do have a freedom to serve Christ, especially "in the present distress." A married person fears death or imprisonment, not necessarily because of his or her own loss, but because of its impact on others.

Would Paul's own ministry have been significantly different if he had been married? Perhaps. We have no way to be certain if Paul was ever married, but by the time he wrote to the Corinthians, he was definitely single. Whether by intuition and observation or through experience, Paul knew that marriage changes the way a person thinks, even a Christian who really loves the Lord.

Living It Out

Verse 35 is the key to Paul's whole line of argument. His purpose is not to lay unbearable burdens and ascetic restrictions on single believers, but to give them a principle for making the right decision. The phrase translated "not to put a restraint on you" literally means "not to throw a noose on you," indicating that Paul desperately wanted to avoid some slavish, legalistic rule that might be used as a test of devotion. So, he gives a guideline "to promote what is proper . . . so that you may be devoted to the Lord without distraction."

At the very least, Christians contemplating marriage should ask themselves whether they can still be true to their calling and fair to their spouse at the same time. While not impossible, devotion to the Lord and faithfulness to a spouse may at times be the greatest challenge that a believer will face. The concerns of this life are inevitable, but commitment to Christ must have first place.

Make God Your Priority in Exercising Control

1 Corinthians 7:36–40

The Big Picture

Paul's argument in 1 Corinthians 7 seems to have touched many subjects, but the Christocentric lens through which he looks at each of them has not changed. Christ is Lord, and Christians must use their social station in life or marital status, whatever it may be, to serve and glorify him. In today's passage he gives some concluding advice to singles, focusing primarily on exercising self-control and maintaining sexual purity. Singles who have never married and widows alike face unique temptations, and God's Word provides the way for purity (cf. Ps. 119:9). To navigate these challenges faithfully, we must receive the godly advice laid out for us in 1 Corinthians 7.

Digging In

The remaining five verses of this chapter divide naturally into two parts. First Corinthians 7:36–38 focus on behavior during engagement while the last two verses address widows. Though such individuals may be at very different stages of life and experience, they are united by their faith in Christ and the exhortation to make God the priority in the way they deal with their need for companionship.

Paul begins in chapter 7, verse 36 by addressing engaged couples, particularly the men. His phrasing sounds peculiar to modern ears, but he is only reiterating his previous teaching in a more direct way. If a couple is engaged and the young man finds it ever more difficult to restrain himself, Paul assures him that going ahead and marrying her is no sin. Knowing the Corinthians' tendency to overemphasize a single biblical teaching and render it out of balance, he repeats that, as beneficial as singleness and celibacy may be, marriage is good and right in the eyes of God.

This is perfectly consistent with the advice he already gave in chapter 7, verse 9: "But if they do not have self-control, they should marry, since it is better to marry than to burn with desire." Paul is neither blind nor unrealistic about the natural, God-given passion that can exist between a young man and woman who are engaged. Even though many marriages were arranged in the first century, couples often got to know one another during the period of betrothal and fell in love. Knowing that one will spend the rest of one's life with this person opens the door to envisioning a sexual relationship, which in turn feeds the desire. Paul shows neither shock nor shame at a man having sexual desire for his fiancé. In fact, there may be a problem if they *don't* feel it. Sexual desire is part of God's good design, and only sinful when satisfied outside of the parameters of marriage that he has established.

So, to any engaged couple feeling that sexual tension, Paul counsels, "He can do what he wants." By no means does that grant permission for a Christian couple to go ahead and have intercourse. Paul clarifies what he means by adding, "They can get married." This is a case in which their marriage would actually help them render undistracted devotion to the Lord rather than remaining single and burning with passion. On the other hand, if a man and his intended bride can continue their engagement for a longer period without undue strain on their relationship to the Lord and to one another, he "will do well" (7:37) to keep her as his fiancé until the time they intend to marry. He does better, in fact, because he has more control over his desires.Purity and passion are not only difficult to balance for young people, but also for widowed persons. Paul applies the same logic to those who are single again as he did to their younger counterparts. If a widow remarries, his only inviolable restriction is that she must marry "only in the Lord" (7:39). Even years of marital experience cannot save her from all the sorrows that derive from an unequal yoke. Though a widow is completely free from her first marriage and has the liberty to remarry within the faith, Paul thinks that she will be "happier" to remain single. Paul's advice in this passage seems to be directed primarily to older widows, because in his first epistle to Timothy, Paul writes, "Therefore, I want younger women to marry, have children, manage their households, and give the adversary no opportunity to accuse us" (1 Tim. 5:14).

Even here, he openly gives this as his "opinion" (1 Cor. 7:40) because he is happy. Earlier in the chapter he admitted that he enjoyed his single status so much that "I wish that all people were as I am," but he gladly conceded that "each has his own gift from God" (7:7). In this instance, when he gives his opinion that a widow remains single, he adds, "And I think that I also have the Spirit of God." These words are not so much a part of his admonition to widows as they are his signature on the entire discussion of chapter 7. Paul is aware of the Corinthian emphasis on the Spirit and the gifts. This is another defense of his apostleship and claim to authority.

Living It Out

Whether single or married, young or old, the main principle that Paul drives home is that God's children must make all their decisions based on their devotion to God. Whether one exercises self-control through celibacy or through marriage, either status requires self-discipline and a commitment to Christ that supersedes selfish concerns. When Paul says,

"I also have the Spirit of God," he is providing a personal testimony that the Spirit of God has been sufficient for him. He has faced the same desires and temptations that the rest of us face, but the Holy Spirit has been with him the whole time, enabling him to make God the priority in the face of crisis, circumstances, concerns, and control. Though we do not have the Spirit giving us apostolic authority as he gave to Paul, we have the same Spirit and the same power enabling us to choose the best and to establish God as our great priority of life.

How to Enjoy
Christian Liberty

1 Corinthians 8:1–13

The Big Picture

The depth of division and acrimony in the Corinthian church has been obvious from the beginning of the letter, and now a new source of dissonance emerges. At the heart of Paul's answer lies a path for Christians to settle disputes on matters about which the Scriptures do not speak directly. Specifically, how can Christians live in a non-Christian world and maintain holiness while still building relationships with unbelievers and participating in cultural norms? Most importantly, what happens when well-intentioned Christians reach different conclusions about what behaviors are acceptable? The occasion that prompted this chapter was a dispute about whether the Corinthians could eat meat that had been sacrificed to pagan idols, but the principles that Paul provides as a response apply to cultural and religious issues that churches have faced as the church expanded throughout the world. This chapter has four main movements that express the argument: with knowledge, have love (1 Cor. 8:1–3); with doctrine, have patience (8:4–7); with liberty, have sensitivity (8:8–11); and with maturity, have restraint (8:12–13).

Digging In

The Corinthians had written Paul a letter that mentioned several specific matters that warrant the apostle's response. The phrase translated "Now about" in 8:1, also occurring in 7:1, 12:1, 16:1, and 16:12, is Paul's way to introduce a subject that they had written about to him. The abrupt change of topics at each of those sections indicates that he followed the pattern of their letter and answered their questions one by one. After the lengthy discussion of marriage, divorce, remarriage, singleness, and widowhood, Paul moves on to this ostensible clash of Christian liberty and an offended conscience.

In the Greco-Roman world, pagan idolatry often celebrated and observed connections between sacrifices and sexuality as well as between food and fertility. No doubt many Christians wanted to avoid any connection whatsoever with idolatrous practices because of such connotations. The flash point for the Corinthian believers was a disagreement about the appropriateness of participation in eating meat from an animal that had been sacrificed to a pagan deity and going into a pagan temple for a ritualistic meal. The problem was particularly acute because almost all meat sold in the marketplace, particularly in a major city like Corinth, came from sacrificial animals that had been slaughtered at temple ceremonies.

Jewish believers would certainly be reluctant to have anything to do with such meat, and Gentile Christians who had been saved out of idolatry may feel a strong aversion to anything that reminded them of the spiritual darkness of their past. Within the church, however, developed two distinct groups with very divergent convictions about the matter. On the one hand were those who claimed deep spiritual insight, a "knowledge" that, since they knew those gods don't actually exist, they were freed from the concerns of the other group, the "weak" whose consciences were scandalized at the notion of partaking of anything connected to paganism.

"We know that we all have knowledge" seems to be one of the slogans that the first group used to defend their liberty. In a style by now characteristic to this epistle, Paul answers their slogan with a "Yes, but . . ." Paul does not deny their "knowledge." In fact, he has already expressed gratitude that they were enriched by Christ "in all knowledge" (1:5), but he forcefully argues that the love of God, not their knowledge, must be the deciding factor. The point he will make throughout the chapter is that knowledge, untampered by love, is harmful. It "puffs up."

Christians realize that the only God who exists is the God of the Old Testament who has revealed himself through the person and work of Jesus Christ (8:6). The Greek God, Poseidon, lord of the sea, for example, was the patron god of Corinth, and much of the meat in the marketplace would have been sacrificed in his name. But since "an idol is nothing in the world" (8:4), should it trouble a mature Christian to eat a goat that had been sacrificed to him? In 8:4–6 Paul acknowledges that this "knowledge" is correct, but he also reminds them that some Christians, especially new converts who "have been so used to idolatry up until now," do not have this knowledge and would be scandalized to partake in anything related to the false religion out of which they had been saved. To eat it would "defile" their "weak" conscience (8:7).

For Paul, a strict Jew and a Pharisee, to argue that "food will not bring us close to God" (8:8) was a remarkable testimony of his own conversion. Much of the Mosaic law and daily Jewish life involves what may or may not be eaten and under what circumstances. The new covenant, however, has done away with all religious dietary restrictions (see Acts 10:9–16; 11:1–18). As a result, Paul equally applies the converse argument, that food cannot take a believer away from God either (1 Cor. 8:8). The issue, in fact, is not about one's relationship to God but rather to one's "brother or sister for whom Christ died" (8:11). Though Christians might have complete freedom in Christ to do something, they must account for the effects of their actions on weaker, less mature Christians who could possibly be "ruined" by misunderstanding or led back into the behaviors and beliefs of the past.

Interestingly, Paul does not simply answer the question about eating meat by affirming that Christians can indeed partake—though he does say that. He goes beyond the issue of whether one *can* to whether one *should*. If a believer's freedom to partake in an activity that is not inherently sinful might lead a more immature believer into sin or scandal, then the correct course of action is to abstain. Even if the action is not inherently sinful, it can become sinful by its toxic effects if one for whom Christ died is "ruined" and led astray (8:12). To sin against one for whom Christ died is to sin against Christ himself (8:12). Paul's willingness to become a vegetarian rather than to hurt a weaker brother is not just admirable, therefore, but standard behavior for a Christian.

Living It Out

The Christian life is not only lived vertically and legally, with regard for God and what is right or wrong, but also horizontally and relationally, with regard for other believers and what is helpful and *best*. No liberty a believer may enjoy is worth the harm that it might inflict on someone who lacks the maturity to resist the temptation that might come with the freedom.

The gospel is the antidote to legalism *and* licentiousness. Paul rejects both outright in this chapter as throughout the epistle. No mere *thing*—food in this case—can either make anyone closer to or farther from God. Many legalistic forms of Christianity desperately need to learn this. Only Christ can cleanse us from sin and bring us to God. All the religious restrictions in the world cannot make us holy. We are "sanctified in Christ Jesus" (1:2). On the other hand, Christian liberty is never a license to sin, but even more, it cannot be an excuse to disregard the effects actions might have on others.

To be clear, Paul is not giving Christians a trump card that they can play to force others to conform to their sensitive conscience. No one has the right to say to another Christian, "You cannot do X because it offends me," particularly believers who have been saved and in the church for years. They can hardly claim to be "weaker" after following Christ for years. Paul instructs each believer to consider his or her own actions, not to limit the actions of others. Nor is the apostle merely protecting the *feelings* of immature believers who may not like something. Rather, he is concerned about the erosion of their own resolve to continue the way of Christ. If someone saved out of paganism finds returning to the temple for a meal a spiritual comfort, they could be led astray.

Few Western Christians struggle with whether to eat meat that someone sacrificed to an idol, yet this chapter is as relevant today as it was in the Roman world of the first century. A person redeemed by Christ must not insist on rights and freedoms that might cause someone else to fall into sin.

Day Twenty-Three

Laying Aside Rights for the Gospel's Sake

1 Corinthians 9:1–27

The Big Picture

After insisting that believers should consider the impact their decisions and deeds have on others, Paul immediately precludes the objection that would be in the minds of many readers: "But I have the *right* to eat what I want!" Even the redeemed human heart resists giving up those things to which it feels entitled. Paul requires a lot of them when he insists that they should be willing to give up something rather than to cause someone to stumble. Yielding the right to eat meat when a weaker brother's conscience is at stake is a selfless act, but Paul reminds the Corinthians that he asks nothing of them that he has not modeled. He has lived and ministered before them like this from the beginning. He enumerates many rights that he has relinquished so he could bring the gospel to them and offer it without any strings attached. More than an occasional decision, surrendering his rights for the sake of the gospel defines his ministry and directs his most personal daily disciplines.

Digging In

In his epistles, Paul frequently and fervently defended his apostleship (cf. Gal. 1:1, 11–24; 2 Cor. 10–11) because he had been called by God and had seen the risen Christ just like the other apostles, yet he never used his apostolic authority to claim any personal advantage, especially monetarily. To the contrary, he reminds the Corinthians that he has never accepted their money, even though he has the right to do so (1 Cor. 9:3–15). He has the right to eat and drink whatever he wants, but he does not (9:4). He has the right to have a wife, but he remains single (9:5). His expenses should be paid just as a soldier's are, but he pays them himself (9:7). His arguments serve as an assertion of his apostleship as well as a model for self-abasement.

Lest anyone fail to appreciate the legitimacy of the rights that Paul relinquishes, he compellingly proves them, marshalling evidence from the Scriptures as well as experience and logic, to affirm that he would be completely entitled to accept their offerings (1 Cor. 9:3–12). God granted that principle in the law of Moses by commanding that an ox should not be muzzled while grinding grain (9:9; Deut. 25:4) and that a priest should live off the sacrificial offerings (9:13; Lev. 6:16–18, 26). Paul and his ministry team, therefore, have every right to be cared for by the Corinthian church that he planted (Acts 18:1–17) just as a vinedresser is entitled to the fruits of his vineyard (9:7), yet he has been guided by a greater principle than demanding his rights and he has set a higher goal than getting earthly things to which he is entitled.

Paul's "boast" (1 Cor. 9:15–16) is not that he is entitled to their care or even that he preached the gospel to them. He is "compelled" to do that whether willingly or not, but his "boast" is that, when he fulfills the call of God willingly, he gets to preach the gospel *freely* and without any strings or need for remuneration. The only reward Paul wants is the gospel itself (9:18). Preaching *is* the reward! Obedience to the will of God is greater reward than any other prize.

In a wonderful twist of phrase, Paul stresses his freedom and his enthusiastic self-surrender to be everyone's servant so that he might win more of them (9:19). The more people who come to know Christ, the more blessings of the gospel he shares. Paul's strategy was to have complete adaptability to Jews and Gentiles alike, to meet them on their own turf, as it were. Though he is no longer under the law, he is willing to keep certain Jewish holidays and traditions (Acts 16:3; 18:18–19), not because he is obligated to keep the law but because he does not want it to keep Jews from listening to his gospel. In the same way, when in Gentile areas, he never refused to eat with them or to partake of what they ate. He did not break the law to win souls, but he certainly knew how to relate to those outside the law (9:20). He accommodated himself to others without compromising his convictions, but also without demanding his rights.

Paul's actions had one shining goal, a single captivating focus: winning people to Christ (9:22–23). Winning others to Christ was everything: motive, means, goal, and reward. This was the prize for which he raced, the crown for which he ran, the reason for his deliberate fight (9:24–26). He wasn't doing anything carelessly, but in a determined, disciplined, denial of self so that he and others might share in the blessings of the gospel. Paul knew of others who turned back and had been "disqualified" (Gr. *adokimos*)—the word he uses in Titus 1:16 to describe those who "claim to know God, but . . . deny him by their works. They are detestable, disobedient, and *unfit* [*adokimos*] for any good work" (italics added). Paul knows he is an apostle who has seen the risen Christ and is called and sent by God, yet he remains so fixed on the finish line that he disciplines his body to "bring it under strict control" so that he is never "disqualified" from the race and reaches the finish line.

Living It Out

For the Christian, personal rights never take precedence over the spiritual need of others, especially their salvation. This runs contrary to the spirit of the age and the cry of contemporary culture. Even many Christians seem more concerned with demanding their privileges than with reaching their neighbors. Paul does not admonish his readers to give up their rights for any cause or in every situation, but only in those where the conscience of a weaker brother or the salvation of someone is at stake.

Two things stand out in this chapter. First, taking the gospel to others is worth *everything*. Believers should share in the clear declaration of Paul, "Woe to me if I do not preach the gospel!" By accepting responsibility to surrender self, showing availability to share Christ, and demonstrating adaptability to save others, we acknowledge that the glory of Jesus and his gospel is worth all we are and all we have. Second, even Paul didn't coast to the end of his ministry. No matter how great his track record, however many he had reached, and despite what he had already suffered, he maintained a disciplined and focused life determined to persevere in faith and works. No Christian ever drifted into obedience or sanctification. The Christian life is a race, an endeavor, a fight—but there's a prize to be won and a crown to wear that is worth everything!

Fleeing Idolatry

1 Corinthians 10:1–22

The Big Picture

The sin of idolatry is particularly deadly, because we become like what we worship. Idolatry is especially insidious because it inexorably leads to so many other sins. When one's heart becomes fixed on anything other than God, other offenses will inevitably follow, and once a Christian is wallowing in sin, assurance of salvation becomes impossible. This passage carries several stern warnings, particularly against spiritual pride and spiritual idolatry, but it also carries a wonderful promise of God's faithfulness and sufficiency.

Paul's statement in 1 Corinthians 9:27 is shocking, to say the least, but it leads him into this next development of his argument. Once he declared that the reason for his intense focus and spiritual discipline was so he would not be "disqualified," he proceeds to instruct his readers on how to avoid that outcome. They should not to take for granted that they will finish the race well. Proving his claims from Scripture, the apostle points to a familiar example from the Old Testament, the Israelites whom Moses led out of Egypt. Though they had every advantage, the reality that they "were struck down in the wilderness" by God is a powerful cautionary tale for anyone who professes Christ. The only proof that one is a genuine believer is perseverance in faith. Those who claim to believe God but nonetheless worship other things and live a life characterized by disobedience reveal that they were never truly following Christ. On the contrary, genuine believers are kept by God (cf. 1:8–9) *and* they keep the faith. Divine preservation and Christian perseverance are not contradictory but are inseparable truths.

Digging In

The Israelites whom God brought out of Egypt had a lot of external things correct—they were Jewish ("our ancestors"), they were miraculously delivered from their bondage, they passed through the Red Sea, and they were led by a pillar of cloud by day and of fire by night. Paul even says they were "baptized into Moses in the cloud and in the sea" (10:1–4). This intentional anachronistic allusion means that, just like baptism in the New Testament publicly identifies one with Christ, the Israelites were externally identified with Moses, their leader, when they figuratively were immersed in the Red Sea when they passed through. In the wilderness they ate manna from heaven, and they drank water from a rock—a rock which typifies *Christ*! Yet despite all that privilege, most of them perished on the journey (10:5) and never saw the Promised Land.

To drive the point home, Paul repeats the word *all* five times in 1 Corinthians 10:1–4, emphasizing the outward spiritual privilege of all "our fathers." They had the right religion: they were Jews. They had the right leadership: they were under the cloud God sent to them. They had the right experience: they passed through the Red Sea! They had the right identification: they were "baptized into Moses." They had the right spiritual food and drink: they ate manna from heaven and drank water from the Rock ("and that rock was Christ!"). "Nevertheless," Paul asserts, God was not pleased with "most of them" and they were "struck down in the wilderness." If having all those external things in order were the basis of pleasing God, they would not have died, but God requires more than the right religion, or the right leader, or the right experience, or the right baptism, or the right food. He requires a right *heart* that has been cleansed by Christ.

Paul then draws four admonitions from this story (10:7–11): (1) don't become *idolaters* (desiring a god other than the One you have); (2) don't commit *sexual immorality* (desiring a person other than the one you have); (3) don't *test Christ* (desiring an outcome of your actions other than the one they yield); and (4) don't *complain* (desiring circumstances other than the ones you have). With the warnings he reminds the Corinthians of the past consequences that God inflicted: "they were struck down in the wilderness," "they died," "they were destroyed by snakes," and "they were killed by the destroyer."

Paul's advice, however, is not that the Corinthians simply should avoid these sins, as if that alone were confirmation of salvation. The key to the passage is in 1 Corinthians 10:6: "Now these things took place as examples for us, so that we *will not desire evil* things as they did" (italics added). Outward actions always spring from inner reality. Sins emanate from a heart that *desires* evil, but a heart that is fixed on God desires *him*! Someone can fake actions, but not desire. Idolatry is desiring, loving, pursuing, or serving anything more than God. True salvation is a change of heart, a change of direction and desire. Paul's clear logic is that if the Israelites, who had all these outward benefits, still had inner evil desires as evidenced by their actions and judged by God, then that could be true of some professing believers today. He sums up his exposition of this spiritual disaster with a grave caveat: "So whoever thinks he stands must be careful not to fall" (10:12).

Frankly, if the passage ended there, we would be left despondent and in despair, assuming assurance in salvation an impossibility. Thankfully, Paul follows the somber word of caution with a calming word of confidence in 1 Corinthians 10:13. No temptation is unique, as though no one else has faced it before. We can have comfort knowing that other believers have faced the same circumstances and found grace to withstand it. In fact, while our perseverance is cause for discipline and determination, *God's* faithfulness to us, not our faithfulness to him, makes it possible. We will never face a temptation that is too great for us to withstand. Since he always provides a way for us to escape sin through his all-sufficient grace, he is never culpable, and we can never say that we were helpless. The blood of Christ and the indwelling power of the Holy Spirit are always available to the believer in the war with the world, the flesh, and the devil.

God's grace is not supplied to us passively, however, as though defeating sin is automatic or easy. In the relentless onslaught of temptation, genuine believers must actively avail themselves of God's promised grace and "flee from idolatry" (10:14). This simple command is the admonition that all of chapters 8–10 have been driving toward. Fleeing requires running *from* temptation and running *to* Christ. Paul illustrates this through the picture of communion, which is a repeated reminder that faith is all of grace and mercy. The miracle of Christian faith is that our "participation" in Christ is not because of a sacrifice that we have offered, but because of Christ's offering of his own flesh and blood. The Lord's Supper reminds us that we can only share in salvation because we share in what he did for us.

Returning to the issue of meat sacrificed to idols, Paul acknowledges that the issue is not the meat or even the idol, but the idolatrous intent of the one making the sacrifice (10:19–20). Pagan gods don't exist, but demons do! Ultimately, all idolatry is demonic. Paul offers a stark choice. At the table of Christ, we receive mercy, but at the table of idols one finds only condemnation. Feast with Christ or dine with demons, but don't try to do both. Consequently, God will either be a gracious host or a jealous judge.

Living It Out

Living in fellowship with Christ precludes two terrible alternatives: (1) the kind of spiritual pride that treats God's grace as an entitlement to sin, and (2) the gripping fear that we can never be accepted by God and assured of eternal life. Outward obedience is important. Baptism, communion, church membership all matter, but they cannot *save.* Israelites who walked through miraculously parted waters, ate bread from heaven, and drank water that Christ provided still perished under the judgment of God because their hearts were never directed toward him. Professing Christians cannot trust in outward acts of obedience alone for evidence of salvation. Desiring God from the heart and walking in fellowship with him is the continuing assurance that we are his and share in the life of his Son.

Living a Life That Glorifies God

1 Corinthians 10:23–11:1

The Big Picture

Liberty in Christ is a marvelous benefit of salvation, yet even that wonderful blessing has limitations, especially when its expression might hinder the conscience or even the salvation of another person. In this passage, Paul continues the line of discussion that he began in chapter 8 about surrendering rights and provides guidelines for knowing how to choose between what is good and what is *best*, between what is permissible and what is *advisable*. In a world filled with ungodly influences, Christians frequently face cultural issues and practices with unsavory origins. Knowing when to abstain and when to participate is essential. The key, according to Paul, is found in having the right intent of serving others and glorifying God.

Digging In

Throughout 1 Corinthians Paul frequently responds to something that the Corinthians have said or written to him in a letter. They embraced several simplistic slogans that Paul felt the need to answer with a "Yes, but . . ." type of response. Their half-true slogans included things like "It is good for a man not to use a woman for sex" in 1 Corinthians 7:1 (author's paraphrase). Obviously that refrain needed a lot of clarification because it's true in some circumstances, but not universally so. The same applies to "Everything is permissible for me" which occurs twice in 6:12 and is repeated twice more here in 10:23. Paul is very concerned lest that slogan become an excuse to permit *everything*, including sin and hurting someone else.

The question, according to Paul, is not "May I?" but rather "Should I?" Even if something is "permissible" for a believer, it may not be "beneficial" (10:23). Notably, Paul does not even accept a choice between good things and bad things. That choice was already made for a Christian the moment Christ entered her heart as Savior and Lord. Even in matters that are not inherently sinful, three questions need to be asked: Is it expedient? Is it edifying? Is it encouraging? But the object of these criteria is not for benefit for self, but rather for *others*. "No one is to seek his own good, but the good of the other person" (10:24). The divisions in the church at Corinth that he has already addressed testify that they have not been living an other-centered life.

As a test case, Paul returns to the issue of eating meat that has been sacrificed to a pagan deity and then sold in the marketplace. The apostolic permission to eat such meat could not be clearer: "Eat everything that is sold in the meat market, without raising questions for the sake of conscience" (10:25). A vegan or vegetarian diet is not necessarily wrong, according to Paul, but a Christian cannot argue for it on moral grounds. Christians are free to eat meat regardless of its origins. This liberty is rooted in God's lordship over all creation (Ps. 24:1 cited in 1 Cor. 10:26). Paul, therefore, frees up the Corinthian believers from a troubled conscience over being invited to eat with unbelievers, a situation that they must face frequently. Eating meat sacrificed to a false god, even with someone who worships that false god, is perfectly permissible for a believer because *the redeemed know better*! The mature believer knows the one true God. Why should someone else's erroneous belief and misguided intent warrant the abstinence of one who knows better?

On the other hand, Paul charges that if a mature believer is a guest at such a meal and another believer, presumably the "weaker brother" of 1 Corinthians 8:9–13, says, "This is food from a sacrifice," hinting that they are scandalized by it, then don't eat it (10:28) to avoid bringing offense to that person's conscience. Even though the other person is "weak" and immature because he does not have a deeper understanding of God's grace and lordship over all creation, anything that is not of faith is sin (Rom. 14:23), and it would be harmful to lead someone whose conscience is bothered to violate their integrity and partake.

Even though Christians should be sensitive to the conscience of others and willing to surrender the right to participate, they should not go so far as to yield their own conscience and conviction. The decision to abstain from some activity out of loving concern for a brother or sister should not be confused with having one's own conscience bound. In fact, Paul demands precisely the opposite. Don't give up your soul's liberty even when you choose to refrain physically. "I do not mean your own conscience, but the other person's" (1 Cor. 10:29a). The Christian who enjoys freedom most is the one who surrenders rights because of love without also surrendering liberty because of fear (10:29–30).

Paul concludes the section with three straightforward commands. First, do everything for the glory of God (10:31). That motive serves as the plumb line for all other decisions. Second, avoid any offense that might keep someone from coming to faith in Christ (10:32–33). When we assert our rights, we make it about ourselves, but when the pure motive of reaching the lost with the gospel saturates our minds, the only benefit we desire is to see others saved. Finally, Paul tells the Corinthians to follow him as he follows Christ (11:1). Christian discipleship is like the children's game, Follow the Leader. We only have the right to expect others to follow us to the degree that we are following Christ. When we are following him closely, we can safely urge others to follow our example. Christ laid aside his divine prerogatives and made himself a servant (Phil. 2:5–11). We could have no better motive nor model to follow than him.

Living It Out

Edification and evangelism are the twin motives of Christian behavior toward others. We must never allow our conscience to be bound by someone else because they do not have the liberty that we enjoy, but our desire to see them follow Christ should always outweigh our demand to exercise our freedoms. Similarly, we should not waste time telling lost people how offended we are by their behavior. Paul urged the Corinthians neither to be scandalized by the sacrifices of their pagan neighbors nor to avoid eating with them. When our motive toward God is his glory and our desire for others is their salvation, we will make our decisions with humility and our actions with grace.

Day Twenty-Six

Men and Women in Worship

1 Corinthians 11:2–16

The Big Picture

Throughout this epistle Paul addresses issues and problems in the church that have erupted in division and diminished the church's effectiveness in evangelism and discipleship. When a church is dysfunctional and divided when it gathers for worship, it will be hobbled and hopeless in nearly every other ministry. When Christians cannot worship in unity and order, they will not find accord in activity or even doctrine. The situation becomes even more dire when that disunity begins in the homes of the church members and spills over into the worship because then *both* institutions, the home and the church, fail to display the character of God. In chapters 8–10, Paul has instructed the Corinthians about their liberty in Christ and the marvelous freedom that it brings, but he has also taken great care to teach them when self-limitation on that liberty is the better course of action.

In the pagan context of Corinth, women were perpetually dishonored and demeaned. They were not considered citizens and were often subject to mistreatment and abuse from their husbands. Christianity brought a liberating ethic of honor for women as equal to men in value, in access to God, and as divine image-bearers. That new freedom did not, however, erase all distinctions and differences. In 1 Corinthians 11:2–16, Paul appeals to the divine order in the Godhead as a model for an order of authority in the home and in the public worship. While this passage presents several interpretative and applicational challenges, the overall meaning is clear.

Digging In

When Paul commends the church because they "hold fast to the traditions just as I delivered them to you," he is not merely thanking them for past obedience, but urging them to remain faithful and, as it becomes more evident, politely suggesting that they actually need to return to those practices. What follows reveals that they are beginning to depart from Paul's instructions. To call them back to the right theology of worship and of the home, he begins with a lesson in theology proper and takes his readers into the very nature of the triune God.

The theological issue at the heart of their disunity is *headship*. While the word "head" might be interpreted several ways in different contexts, Paul leaves little question about what he means by the word. He either uses it literally to mean the head on the body or he uses it figuratively to mean "one who is of supreme or pre-eminent status, in view of authority."[14] In fact, linguistic scholars J. P. Louw and E. A. Nida translate verse 3 as "Christ is supreme over every man, the husband is supreme over his wife, and God is supreme over Christ.[15] Whatever else Paul may be saying in this passage about specific actions, he clearly bases it on the order of authority in the Godhead, in humanity, and in the home. Christ willingly submits to the Father as his authority even though they are coequal, coeternal, and coexistent. Headship does not and cannot connote superiority because God the Father is the "head" of God the Son. Even though God has given these structures of authority in the church and the home, they should be sources of unity and joy, not domination and abuse. A husband should strive with all his might to be a "head" to his wife as Christ is lovingly, sacrificially, and righteously a "head" of the man. The manner and spirit by which a husband leads should reflect the headship under which he lives and to which he submits.

In 1 Corinthians 11:4–5 the apostle denounces two ways that both men and women shame their "heads" in public worship: men when they pray with their heads covered and women when they pray or prophesy with their heads *un*covered. Though many scholars believe this passage is referring to hair styles (men with long hair and women leaving their hair down), it seems more likely that Paul is referring to wearing an artificial covering of some kind when he refers to women because of verse 6: "But if a woman doesn't cover her head, she should have her hair cut off." The word for "covering" in verse 15 is a different word than Paul has been using throughout the passage, indicating that he has two different kinds of coverings in mind.

Putting all underlying exegetical difficulties aside, one can easily discern the main point Paul is making. His argument is that God designed the distinction between men and women and that this distinction should not be eradicated in the church. Women in the Greco-Roman world of the first century always covered their heads—temple prostitutes (who were not under the authority of a husband) were a noteworthy exception. Apparently, some Corinthian women, now understanding their equality in Christ, threw off their head coverings and came to worship uncovered. Paul points out that this departure from the cultural norm was dishonoring to their heads, their husbands. If a man wore a covering like a woman, this was dishonoring to his head, Christ. This instruction logically follows his previous arguments about surrendering rights for the sake of others. Even though believing women might be *free* to go without their covering—it's not inherently sinful—they should be willing to surrender that right because of its effect on their husbands as well as a culture that would not understand their departure from societal norms.

One other interpretative difficulty is worth noting. Paul tells women to wear the symbol of authority "because of the angels" (11:10). Knowing precisely why the angels matter in this context is complicated, to say the least, but the best explanation, at least to the simple mind of this author, is that angels are connected to the worship of the Lord (Isa. 6:3; Rev. 5:11; Job 38:7; Ps. 148:2). They attend the worship of the church and desire to "catch a glimpse of" gospel matters (1 Pet. 1:12). Since humans are created "a little lower than the angels" (Ps. 8:5) and are fallen recipients of God's grace and forgiveness through Christ—which is never true of fallen angels—holy angels must be scandalized by the absence of order and authority in worship. Angels desire to see God worshiped and his authority structures honored. Since believers will one day judge the angels (6:3), they ought to be respectful of their presence now.

Living It Out

One thing is clear from this chapter. Headship exists within the Trinity, within the home, and within the church. To deny that renders this chapter pointless and meaningless. Paul cautioned that the Corinthian women should not use their liberty in Christ to throw off the symbols of their husband's headship. Coverings were recognized in that culture as appropriate for married women and to refuse them when speaking to God in public prayer or for God through a prophetic utterance was scandalous to the culture at large, to their husbands, and even to angels. Men, too, should be distinctly male and not wear a covering during prayer.

A head covering is not considered particularly masculine or feminine in Western culture today, but the point Paul makes in 1 Corinthians 11:2–16 remains. Christian men and women should respect God-given authority structures and reflect their distinctive masculinity and femininity respectively. Husbands should lead their wives and participate in public worship in a way that reflects Christ as their head. The appearance of wives should be distinctively feminine in a way that honors Christ, respects their husbands, and testifies even to the angels. Though cultural norms that reflect gender and headship may change through time and place, the principle of order in worship as a reflection of God's character should be reflected in every church everywhere.

Day Twenty-Seven

Community and Communion

1 Corinthians 11:17–34

The Big Picture

At the heart of much of the division in the church at Corinth, as is usually the case, lay a self-centeredness that undermined the gospel Paul had preached to them. Consequently, throughout the epistle the apostle has been steadily chiseling away at a Christianity that emphasizes rights over responsibilities, freedom over faithfulness, and rules over relationship. Nowhere did their egocentrism present itself more shockingly than in their fractured observance of the Lord's Supper. In 1 Corinthians 11:17–22 Paul presents his complaint against them and enumerates the abuses of communion that have been reported to him. In verses 22–26 he shares the pattern of observance of the Supper that Jesus had instituted, reminding them of its significance. Finally, in verses 27–34 he provides very specific instructions about the proper way to observe this special meal and warns of the severity with which God judges those who partake in an unworthy manner.

Digging In

In 1 Corinthians 11:2 Paul commended the church for the way
they had remembered his teaching and kept the traditions he had delivered to them, but he begins this section with a stark reversal by bluntly
declaring that he has no praise for the way the church has fractured
and allowed factions to segregate the church. In fact, their gathering
actually did more harm than good (11:17). With a nod back to his
earlier rebuke for following different leaders (3:1–9), he notes the irony
of having "divisions" when "you come together" (11:18). If they have
divided themselves into factions, of course, then they don't really "come
together." As was often the case, they celebrated what they should have
mourned (5:2) and believed that the factions were necessary to recognize the members among them who had distinguished themselves by
being "approved" (11:19).

The Corinthians had apparently conflated their church dinners
with their observance of the Lord's Supper, and the result was that, not
only did they observe the Supper incorrectly, they didn't even observe
it *together*, an error so serious that Paul refuses to allow them to call it
"the Lord's Supper" (11:20). Their erroneous practice meant it belonged
to *them*, not to Christ. Some members arrived early and ate and drank
everything, even to the point of drunkenness, leaving nothing for the
others who came later. This selfish display meant that (1) they weren't
really fulfilling the ordinance that Jesus had given his church; (2) they
were despising God's church and acting as if it were theirs; and (3) they
were humiliating the people who had nothing and could not arrive as
early. Such behavior received no word of praise or commendation from
Paul.

Paul returns to the basics, reminding the church of what he had
"received from the Lord" and previously "passed on" to them (11:23),
which they had summarily disregarded. When Jesus broke the bread
and took the cup, he emphasized that the Supper was completely and
distinctly about *him*, not *them*. "This is my body . . . Do this in remembrance of me . . . my blood . . . Do this . . . in remembrance of me"
(11:24–25). The purpose of the Lord's Supper is "to proclaim the Lord's
death until he comes" (11:26), but the gluttonous manner in which they

childishly raced to devour it and engorge themselves eradicated any semblance of the spirit in which Christ intended it to be observed. One cannot help but remember that the disciples had themselves fallen into this trap when, no sooner than Jesus had served them, a dispute arose among them about which of them was the greatest (Luke 22:14–30). Few things indicate the depth of human sinfulness more than perverting an opportunity to express gratitude for God's grace into an occasion for selfish pride.

The specific vocabulary used in this description of the Lord's table reflects the three tenses of salvation. "In remembrance of me" refers to the past, recalling the historic event of Christ's death that believers appropriated when they trusted Christ. "You proclaim the Lord's death" emphasizes the present purpose of the ordinance as a visual preaching of the gospel. "Until he comes" points the participants to the future banquet in the Kingdom that they will observe with Jesus himself (Luke 22:14–18) when the *eschaton* is realized.

In his final instructions about the proper observance of the Supper, Paul notes that the only individual aspect (as opposed to the corporate) is self-examination (1 Cor. 11:28). To proclaim the Lord's death through the symbols of his flesh and blood is a profound and momentous duty. It requires coming to the Lord's table in repentance, gratitude, and a right relationship to others in the body. To participate in communion "without recognizing the body" is to "eat and drink judgment" to oneself (11:29). Paul stresses that the Corinthians have experienced illness and even death in their church because God has judged some of them for their disrespect of his table and what it signifies. His admonition is that either we will judge ourselves and come to the Supper in the proper way or else we will be "disciplined" by the Lord lest we be "condemned with the world," a reminder of the dire warning of 10:12. Those who can repeatedly partake of the Lord's Supper with no thought for their betrayal of its sacred purpose or for their own spiritual state do not pass the test and prove themselves disqualified (9:27).

The proper observance of the Lord's Supper demands that they be assembled together so they can "welcome one another" (11:33) and that they not treat the Lord's Supper as if it were intended to satiate their fleshly appetites. That normal kind of hunger should be satisfied at home (11:34) and spare them from the judgment that selfish attitudes and actions bring. The table of communion satisfies a different kind of hunger, the believer's need for fellowship in the gospel and participation in the body of Christ.

Living It Out

Not many Christians take the observance of the Lord's Supper as seriously as this passage demands. Perhaps one reason so many churches are anemic and ineffective is that, though they may not abuse it as overtly as the Corinthian church, they have nonetheless made it about themselves rather than about Christ. The Lord's Table is intended as an enactment of the gospel. Just as salvation required repentance with faith, so should believers forsake sin, past and planned, as they outwardly picture the reality that they have appropriated to themselves the Lord's body and blood. Furthermore, communion is not intended as a private enterprise for the purpose of giving communicants a warm, comfortable feeling, but rather as a public declaration of the death of Jesus, a death required by a righteous God as an atonement for the sins of those who have participated in that sacrifice by faith.

Spiritual Gifts

1 Corinthians 12:1–11

The Big Picture

Chapter 12 commences a major section of 1 Corinthians that continues through chapter 14. At first glance the division seems to be about the use of *charismata*, or spiritual gifts—and it is—but on deeper inspection Paul is educating them about much more than how to *use* their gifts. He is constructing a *theology* of spiritual gifts that is consonant with everything he has written in the epistle to this point. Building on his previous comments about the gospel, divisions, surrendering rights, self-restraint, idolatry, seeking God's glory, authority structures, and self-examination, he settles in to tackle the issue that he has been alluding to since the opening of the letter. Way back in 1:4–7 he shared thanksgiving to God that they were "enriched . . . in all speech and in all knowledge," specifically that they "do not lack any spiritual gift." In those few words, he wisely precluded any argument he might later arouse in the Corinthian church that he resented their spiritual gifts. Like any tool, spiritual gifts are neither good nor bad in themselves. The manner and purpose of their use is what matters, and Paul is going to locate their utilization in the lordship of Christ, the intent of the Spirit, and the function of the local church.

Digging In

The "Now concerning" in 12:1 is a discourse marker that announces Paul's shift of subject, but also seems to indicate previous discussion, perhaps in their letter to him. It becomes clear in the following verses that their misuse of the gifts spawned division and disturbance in the church, particularly in their worship. Legitimate Christian spiritual gifts (Gr. *charismata*) closely resembled certain pagan practices in the Greco-Roman world of the first century, and Paul alludes to that when he reminds them of their idolatrous past (12:2). One of the best-known examples would be the oracle of Apollo at Delphi, in Greece. From all over the Mediterranean world, people would journey to Mount Parnassus to pose questions of the Pythia, a woman who would answer in ecstatic utterances, presumably from Apollo, that the priests would then "interpret" for the paying supplicant. This cultural milieu would have been very well known to every citizen of Corinth and a significant part of the religious background of the members of the church prior to their conversion.

Paul begins with the most basic test of any supernatural gift. Can the speaker affirm that Jesus is Lord? No demonic spirit could do that just as no Christian would dare breathe the words, "Jesus is cursed! (12:2–23). The most basic test of gifts is that they are subject to the lordship of Christ.

Though the gifts, ministries, and activities of the Spirit display tremendous diversity, they reflect a distinct unity in their origin and purpose. The ground of that unity is the triune God himself named in verses 4–6 by the words "Spirit" (Gr. *pneuma*), "Lord" (Gr. *kurios*), and "God" (Gr. *theos*). These spiritual gifts come from the one God as a "manifestation of the Spirit" (12:7). This would be a radically different perspective than the polytheism of Corinth, which claimed that different patron gods bestowed unique skills on their respective worshipers. In contrast, the purpose of the gifts of the Spirit, "the common good" (12:7b) is as crucial as their source. Paul is brilliant at almost casually or imperceptibly laying out threads of truth that he will take up later and weave into the context of his larger logical argument. Much of chapter

14 will reassert this claim and reason that if a gift cannot be used for the common good, it should not be used at all.

In 1 Corinthians 12:8–10, Paul lists different types of *charismata* that prove the wide range of the grace gifts given to individuals in the church. Some do not necessarily seem supernatural—like wisdom, knowledge, and faith, though, in fact, they are. Unbelievers can have natural wisdom, knowledge, and faith in the human dimension, but only the Holy Spirit can grant these in ways that overcome the mental and spiritual effects of the fall. Even after salvation believers cannot claim to have perfect understanding of spiritual truths. Especially before the completion of the canon and the availability of the written Scriptures, which Peter called "the prophetic word strongly confirmed" (2 Pet. 1:19), the early church relied on people who had supernatural gifts of insight into truth, knowledge about God, or faith for great works of God. Healing, miracles, prophecy, distinguishing spirits, and tongues may seem more obviously supernatural, but God is always responsible anytime a fallen human being can understand spiritual things.

Paul does not take the time to define these gifts carefully or specifically distinguish between them. He does not explain the difference in a "message of wisdom" or a "message of knowledge," which has not dampened the confidence with which many people attempt it two thousand years later! He's much more concerned that the Corinthians know that all the gifts come from one source and that they all have one purpose. The Holy Spirit is actively distributing the gifts. They are *gifts*, and therefore not earned nor a cause of pride. Furthermore, they do not result from human will but rather the will of the Spirit (1 Cor. 12:11) who is gifting individuals in the church to serve the church "for the common good" and not for the exaltation of pride or even for personal edification.

Living It Out

Few things divide Christians (and even Christianity) quite like their views about spiritual gifts. Entire denominations, let alone churches, have split or formed over these issues. One thing is certain.

Any vitriolic division in a church over spiritual gifts is evidence that they are not being used or received as the Holy Spirit intended. Just as Paul warned the church at Corinth that they could pervert the Lord's Supper and make it belong to them instead of Christ, so can believers abuse the spiritual gifts so that they ultimately have little to do with the Spirit.

Subsequent studies in chapters 12–14 will delve further into the explanation of what the gifts are and what they accomplish in the church, but the primary principle of spiritual gifts must be that they are used for the common good in the context of the church and not for personal satisfaction or pride. Just as the Corinthians had seen pagan practices that closely resembled spiritual gifts, two thousand years later modern believers must not believe everyone who claims to have a gift or ascribe it to the Holy Spirit. We need to apply Paul's trilateral test for ourselves as well as for others: does the gift affirm the lordship of Christ? Is the gift used for the purpose of edifying others? Is the gift exercised within the authority for the unity of a local church?

Day Twenty-Nine

The Body of Christ

1 Corinthians 12:12–31

The Big Picture

First Corinthians 12–14 form a significant unit in 1 Corinthians in which Paul advances a theology of spiritual gifts. Since Paul insists that these gifts function within the church, his *pneumatology*, the doctrine of the Spirit, is closely related to *ecclesiology*, the doctrine of the church. Using the human body as a metaphor, Paul explains how the many different members of the church with their many different gifts and actions all serve the same purpose. In a sense, Christians surrender any right to assert their individualism from the moment of their baptism because that signifies that they identified with Christ in his *death*. Believers die to self to live toward God. Each one is baptized "into one body" but as a particular "part" with a specific function. Jealousy, envy, and pride should be excluded because the Spirit sovereignly chooses to bestow individual gifts as he wills so that the body has every part that it needs. Not only does the Spirit give *gifts* to the church but also establishes and fills *offices*. No member has all the gifts, and no person holds all the offices, but everyone has a function to fulfill. The body achieves maximum effectiveness and satisfaction when every member operates according to the Spirit's gifting and calling.

Digging In

Paul's extended comparison of the church to a human body begins by explaining how individual Christians become a part of that body. Through baptism, believers identify with Christ. First Corinthians 12:13 is an obvious reference back to 10:2 in which Paul described the Israelites passing through the Red Sea as "baptized unto Moses," meaning that they were identified with Moses, their leader. Baptism *always* means identification with something or someone. When Jesus submitted to John's baptism he was not repenting, for he had no sin, but he was *identifying* with John's message of the arrival of the Kingdom. In Acts 19:3 Paul asked the Ephesian disciples "Into (or *unto*) what were you baptized?" This question is meant to probe their understanding and to determine exactly what they identified with, discovering by their answer that they had never identified with Christ and received the Spirit.

Mutual identification with Christ is a unifying principle because whatever background, ethnicity, economic status, or talents one brings, all believers alike come into the church through the waters of baptism. Though, admittedly, some Bible scholars take 1 Corinthians 12:13 as a reference to being baptized in the Spirit into the universal church at the moment of conversion, ordinary water baptism into the local church, which every member willingly experienced and could easily recall, seems the most likely meaning. The gifts are expressed in the context of the local church. The Spirit is the divine agent that leads the believer to follow Christ in baptism, hence, "we are all baptized by one Spirit into one body" and "given one Spirit to drink," a reference back to 10:4 in which the Israelites all drank from the Rock that followed them, which Paul identifies as Christ.

Because a believer owes salvation, gifting, and even baptism to the Spirit, pride has no place in a Christian life. The proper response is to discover and to use the gifts the Spirit has given in a selfless way that promotes the health of the body. Paul develops this reasoning and makes several significant conclusions in 1 Corinthians 14:24a. First, church members have no right to be jealous of the gifts of others and demean their own function because they cannot do what someone else does. The foot does not get to refuse to function because it cannot be the hand. Second, the body needs every member to function within its designed purpose. "If they were all the same part," Paul asks (12:19), "where would the body be?" The purpose of the gifts is wholeness in the body, not fulfillment in the member (12:20). Third, all members need one another and have no right to denigrate the function of others because their gifts are different. Different is not inferior. In a somewhat colorful way, Paul talks about parts of the body that are "weaker" but are indispensable, parts that "we consider less honorable" which "we clothe with greater honor," and even "our unrespectable parts" that "are treated with greater respect."

In other words, a body part that is rarely seen still has a critical function! No one should overinterpret these words and try to make these "unrespectable" body parts mean certain members or jobs in the church, but readers should rather understand Paul's main point that everyone in the church has a purpose and is worthy of being valued by every other member of the church. All manner and levels of gifts that the Spirit has bestowed should be celebrated. Division in the body is contrary to God's purpose in putting the body together (12:24b–25). What happens to one member of the body, good or bad, is felt and shared by all (12:26).

Just as each member has particular gifts, though no one has all of them, so the church has specific offices that God has appointed with no individual able to hold all the offices. Once again, Paul does not define these offices clearly in this passage, but they were clear enough to the Christians of the first century that he did not need to do so. This does not mean that every church had all these represented, but these were indicative of the Spirit's work in supplying the body precisely with what was needed. What they all share is a design for teaching and leadership of the church, particularly before Christians had a completed and written canon, all sixty-six books of the Bible, to guide them. Some of them are gifts of leadership, others are gifts of revelation, still others are supernatural sign gifts. Paul asks seven questions about them (12:29–30), each of which anticipates a negative response and indicates that no one has all these abilities or gifts. There remains, however, one thing—one *more excellent way*—that everyone in the church can have: love (13:1–13).

Living It Out

Though spiritual gifts have been given by the Holy Spirit to unify the church, they have often been misused or misunderstood by individuals to divide what God intended to unify. Christians still disagree over which of these gifts and offices endure even after apostolic age and the completion of the canon. Some Christians and denominations even believe the church today still has apostles. These important questions deserve answers but lie beyond the scope of this study. However definitively we may answer them, we can still run the risk of disregarding the main point on which Paul was insisting. All the gifts and each office, whatever they are and however long they endure, are intended for the good of the body and not for the pride or edification of the individual. All members in the church should work for the health and realization of the whole body, and not for self. Individual expression must always bow to corporate health.

A Love Supreme: Essential and Empowering

1 Corinthians 13:1–7

The Big Picture

In the middle of his very practical discussion and correction to the Corinthians about their misuse of the charismatic gifts, Paul injects some of the most lilting, exuberant, and elevated prose ever written. Birthed in the real world of church conflict, this prose ascends to breathtaking heights of grandeur that transcend any single situation. Sharply practical, and yet soaringly philosophical, too, 1 Corinthians 13 is deservedly one of the best-known and most loved passages of the Bible.

Digging In

In a broad stroke of hyperbole, Paul unflinchingly makes the point that truth without love is meaningless. Many in the Corinthian church had focused on the gift of tongues and had taken pride in a gift that they had not earned and did nothing to deserve. The apostle clearly crafts a statement that will eviscerate their pride and excise the cancer of self-will and self-promotion. The degree of one's giftedness is insignificant compared to the depth of giving oneself. Any gift, regardless of how spectacular or remarkable, is useless without love. The point continues in 1 Corinthians 13:2: no matter how great his spiritual insights through prophetic powers, exegetical insight that demystifies hidden truths, and mountain-moving faith, insight without love is senseless.

Running throughout the entire epistle is an undercurrent of opposition to pride, especially the pride that comes because of one's exalted knowledge. From the identification of an Apollos party in the first chapter to his final bequest of love in the epistle's ultimate verse, Paul constantly urges his Corinthian friends to abandon any pride in their knowledge or spiritual superiority and instead manifest the love of Christ. Many Bible scholars and teachers have forgotten to keep their hearts full as well as their heads.

First Corinthians 13:3, however, cuts much deeper and gets far more personal. Paul shocks his readers that it might even be possible to do the most altruistic acts, the most phenomenal feats of philanthropic performance, the most dramatic deeds of selflessness, only to discover that sacrifice without love is pointless. Paul's poetic warning in verse 3 is completely consistent with his doctrine of salvation by grace alone. The loveless philanthropist can expect no celestial confirmation or heavenly brownie points. Even the most extreme gifts have no merit before God when they are devoid of a divine love that can only be realized as a *result* rather than a *cause* of divine grace.

Unfortunately, many people have an unsustainable view of love. They mistakenly think of it as some nebulous, indefinable wave of emotion that sweeps over a person and manifests itself in irrepressible fashion. Consequently, they may not be able to define it, but they claim that they know it when they see it or, more usually, feel it. For Paul love is not at all vague or difficult to define, nor does it have much to do with feelings. Instead, it has everything to do with acts of the will, the cold, hard rational decision to do the right thing because one has chosen to love.

The apostle's definition of love in these four verses is as beautiful a description and exhortation as has ever been written, but it also exhibits a pragmatic quality that seems to divide into two aspects: the power of love in *character* and in *constancy*.

Verses 4–6 enumerate those ways that love changes our character and shapes our integrity. Love accomplishes what the law cannot: it makes us *want* to be better and do the right thing, to be selfless and centered on others. In a word, love makes us holy. Isn't that the effect of this kind of divine love? When we are patient and kind, never envious or boastful, free from arrogance and rudeness, never insisting on our own way, unencumbered by irritability or resentfulness, delighting ourselves in truth and never in wrongdoing, isn't that the very embodiment of holiness? Is that not the very picture of Christ himself? He was the perfect expression and example of love that Paul holds out as the goal for every believer.

Love will also affect constancy, that ability to persevere and persist, even when love is not returned. First Corinthians 13:7 is a quartet of universal truths that defines true love. Love "bears all things." The depth of one's love will be marked by the height of the pile of things it puts up with. For some, the price of love is too high. They close themselves off from others and ultimately even from God. C. S. Lewis said, "Love anything and your heart will be wrung and possibly broken. If you want to make sure of keeping it intact you must give it to no one, not even an animal. Wrap it carefully round with hobbies and little luxuries; avoid all entanglements. Lock it up safe in the casket or coffin of your selfishness. But in that casket, safe, dark, motionless, airless, it will change. It will not be broken; it will become unbreakable, impenetrable, irredeemable. . . . To love is to be vulnerable."[16] Though he said it much more eloquently, Lewis was merely stating that no one can love without risking hurt and pain, because love will always have a lot of things to bear.

Love "believes all things, hopes all things, endures all things." Love invests itself by trusting, sometimes even when that trust has not yet been earned or has even been violated. We often want a return on an investment never made, a payoff without sacrifice. We expect love to come to us when we haven't given much to others. Even if the reward comes only in heaven, Paul admonishes us to love others with a dogged determination that looks for no exceptions and offers no excuses. This is a commitment to love in "all things."

Living It Out

Unfortunately, what we call "love" is often nothing like the description written in this passage. How many marriages slip into a morass of resentment and irritability? How many children begrudge their parents for past mistakes? Who doesn't know a Christian that has been wounded in the past who still holds a bitter grudge? Love for others should motivate us to desire and strive for the very best for others, even those who have hurt us, and not just for ourselves.

Many people serve without loving. They serve for a paycheck, or for security, or for a warm feeling of accomplishment. No one, however, can love without serving. Servants don't always love, but lovers always serve. Paul admonishes us to examine ourselves to make certain that we have not failed to attain and exhibit the most essential element of the Christian life. It is only when we choose to love that we are truly in control of ourselves. To be bitter, angry, hurt, vengeful, vindictive, or offended is to be controlled by others and by circumstances. The person who can choose to love regardless of the actions of others or the events of life is never a victim, but always a victor. Love is the most empowering act one can ever do.

A Love Enduring

1 Corinthians 13:8–13

The Big Picture

Deep within every human being beats a heart that wants to love and be loved, but our own selfishness wars against the kind of love that Paul writes about in this chapter. Much of what gets called love is not love at all. The world's version of love is often the desire to possess, to control, to manipulate, to feel good, to self-actualize, or simply to lust. The divine love to which God calls us is very different and well defined. The remaining section in this chapter provides a compelling and practical reason to lavish love on others: love lasts when everything else has passed away.

Digging In

The final verses of the chapter remind Paul's audience of the occasion that prompted such poetic expression. The Corinthians were embroiled in controversy, acting selfishly, and filled with pride as a result of their misunderstanding and frequent misuse of the spiritual gifts. The apostle quickly reminds them that the gifts that command their attention and in which they have invested so much emotional energy are temporary and immature niceties, while love is an eternal and essential part of the Christian life.

Paul looks forward to a consummation in which these temporary and immature gifts will no longer be necessary, when something clearer and surer takes its place. "When the perfect comes, the partial will come to an end" (1 Cor. 13:10). The question that we struggle with, of course, is exactly to what does he refer? At what point will prophecies "come to an end," tongues "cease," knowledge "come to an end" (13:8), and the things of childhood finally be "put aside" (13:11) because they no longer suit a mature faith?

Much of the debate centers on Paul's meaning of "the perfect," used to predict the cessation of "the partial." "We know in part and we prophesy in part, but when the perfect comes, the partial will come to an end" (13:9–10). Some believe this refers to the return of Christ, others believe it means the completion of the canon. Frankly, the Holy Spirit could have led Paul to be more specific had he wanted to reveal more than is written here. The only thing we can say with certainty is that nothing in this passage is exegetically conclusive that the spiritual gifts are *either* finished or still present. Though this issue will be discussed in some detail in the following chapter, suffice it to say that by the revelation of the Holy Spirit Paul could look with certainty into an uncertain and two-dimensional future and report confidently that in an unspecified future time of maturity, fulfillment, and clarity, the church would have no need of prophetic utterances, or specially revealed knowledge, or the ability to preach the gospel in previously unknown languages.

On the one hand, love will never end, be passé, or unnecessary, or dull, or out of fashion. Maturity and understanding requires more love, not less. Paul might liken the revelatory gifts to looking into a smoky brass mirror, but he likens the love that comes with maturity to knowing and being known "face to face" (13:12).

The time will come when Christians will no longer need faith. Everything that we have trusted Christ for will be ours and in our possession. In the same way, we will no longer hope, because, as Paul writes elsewhere, "hope that is seen is not hope, because who hopes for what he sees?" (Rom. 8:24). When Christ returns and establishes his kingdom on the earth, his redeemed people will no longer need faith or hope, but "love never ends" (13:8). For now, however, all "these three remain: faith, hope, and love—but the greatest of these is love" (13:13).

Living It Out

I remember the first time I saw my wife. We were at a church party. I was twenty, and she was nineteen. I remember what she wore and how she had fixed her hair when she walked through the door. I looked at my cousin and asked, "Who is *that*?" Two weeks later we had our first date. Two weeks after that we bought her wedding rings, and six months later we were married. We were in love, to be sure, but now, after four decades of marriage, we have grown more deeply and completely in love with one another. Maturation has taught us the difference between what matters and what doesn't, between significance and silliness. We would not trade the sturdy and comfortable bonds that rest so contentedly and effortlessly on our hearts today for that first flush of infatuation and the struggle to learn one another. Passing years have made us grow up, not old.

This is the maturity that Paul longs to see the Corinthian church enjoy. Paul doesn't begrudge the Corinthians the gifts God has given them, nor does he try to make them feel guilty for using them, but he knows that their pride in the gifts is totally misplaced. At best, they are like children proud of their beautiful toys, not realizing that a day will come when they will all be put away in the attic and remembered only in pictures and stories of the past. God's graces of faith, hope, and love are far superior to prophecy, knowledge, and tongues. We don't have to ask if these graces are for today. They *remain*.

But two of them do not abide forever. *Faith* one day will become sight, and we will hold in our hands the things for which we longed and *hoped*, but love will always be *love*. Nothing in eternity will take its place or render it obsolete. No age or dispensation will transcend it. It abides as a permanent marker of Christian existence because of all God's graces extended to man, "the greatest of these is love."

What the Bible Says about Tongues: Part 1

1 Corinthians 14:1–12

The Big Picture

Nothing in the past century has had a greater impact on Christianity than the charismatic movement. Some regard it as demonic, others a distraction, and still others as divine. Since the Azusa Street Revival in 1906, the belief that the miraculous gifts of the apostolic era are still operable today has spread worldwide. Nearly every denomination, Catholicism as well as Protestantism, has some charismatic adherents who believe in ecstatic utterances of tongues, gifts of healing, and ongoing prophetic revelation.

Part of the problem in discussing tongues is agreeing to a definition. Does the gift of tongues refer to speaking a known human language, or an ecstatic utterance—perhaps an angelic language, or both? Good and godly people who desire truth and are deep students of the Word have differences of opinions. With all due respect to those who interpret this differently, this author believes that Acts 2:1–13 defines tongues as the ability to preach the gospel in a human language that the speaker has never learned. The gift of tongues, therefore, is a truly supernatural sign gift that functions as a reversal of the curse of Babel, emphasizing that God is redeeming people from every part of the world and making them one. Furthermore, the gift of tongues was given as a sign so that, as the gospel advanced into new areas, it confirmed the presence of the Kingdom of God as people heard the gospel in their own language.

Not only is defining tongues complicated and controversial, but so also is determining whether the Holy Spirit still gives this gift to individuals today. If so, is the gift for all believers? After all, Paul wrote about the gift tongues in only one of his thirteen epistles, indicating its relative rarity even in the age of the apostles. Any practice of spiritual gifts today, therefore, must be examined in the light of God's Word, and 1 Corinthians 14 is the classic text for any discussion of the charismatic gifts, particularly speaking in tongues.

After the great love chapter in 1 Corinthians 13, Paul transitions from the philosophical and exalted principles into the nuts and bolts pragmatism of chapter 14 by encouraging his readers to "pursue love and desire spiritual gifts" (14:1), especially the superior gift of prophecy. But frankly, the gift of prophecy was not at the center of the Corinthian controversy. The misuse of the gift of tongues was in the eye of the storm. In response, Paul issues four tests that the gift of tongues must pass before it can be accepted as fulfilling its divine purpose. Two of these tests appear in today's study, two others will follow in the chapter 14, verses 13–25.

Digging In

The very first test of any spiritual gift is, "Does it edify the church?" Many have misunderstood verse 2, "the person who speaks in another tongue is not speaking to people but to God" to teach a private prayer language, but that is for self-edification, but Paul is saying exactly the opposite. His description of the Corinthian *misuse* of tongues in verse 2 is antithetical to his prescription for the use of tongues in 14:22, that this gift is "intended as a sign, not for believers, but for unbelievers." The gift of tongues in Acts 2 was inarguably God's gift to the church so they could share the gospel in other languages. Though apparently some in Corinth had originally received the gift of tongues for that purpose, they had begun to use the gift as a mark of pride and God's favor.

This much is indisputable. First, Paul urges the Corinthians to seek revelation rather than mere communication, explaining that prophecy is far superior to tongues. Second, his comment on the self-edification of tongues in verse 2 is contrasted with the church edification of verse 3 and resolved clearly in favor of the superiority of edifying others. Third, though Paul does not say that tongues are wrong, he clearly limits the way that they should be used to serving others (1 Cor. 14:22).

The second test of a spiritual gift is "does it enlighten the listeners?" (14:6–12). Any gift that brings confusion rather than clarity is misused. In rapid succession, Paul gives three examples of the futility of unintelligible sounds: meaningless utterances, lifeless instruments, and a military bugle. After employing these metaphors, Paul uses a final example, which is the situation the Corinthians actually find themselves. They were using the gift of tongues without anyone present who could understand them. Therefore, they were like foreigners, speaking words that contained meaning, but meaning that was lost on the listener because they did not understand that intended meaning. They were zealous to use their gifts, but not zealous "in building up the church" (14:12).

Living It Out

When approaching the subject of speaking in tongues and other spiritual gifts, we must ask ourselves if it edifies the church and enlightens the listeners. However, one understands the nature of this gift, these two tests must be passed before tongues can be accepted as fulfilling its divine purpose.

The *only* time in the New Testament that Christians are told to build themselves up is to build themselves up in the holy faith (Jude 20). In none of the lists of spiritual gifts or offices is self-edification listed as even a secondary purpose of the gifts. Spiritual gifts are given to individuals, but always in the context of the church. A private use of a spiritual gift runs contrary to every New Testament parameter of spiritual gifts.

Paul's conclusion is inescapable. The very purpose of speaking in tongues is to convey *meaning*, and without that conveyance, the gift of tongues was not being used appropriately. Nowhere in these verses does he suggest that they should still use their gift for their own benefit even if no one present understood. To the contrary, they should strive to use their gifts for only one purpose: "building up the church" (1 Cor. 14:12).

What the Bible Says about Tongues: Part 2

1 Corinthians 14:13–25

The Big Picture

In the first part of this chapter, Paul gave two tests that the gift of tongues must pass before it can be accepted as fulfilling its divine purpose: does it edify the church, and does it enlighten the listeners? First Corinthians 14:13–25 expands Paul's correction with the addition of two more tests focusing on understanding (14:13–19) and evangelism (14:20–25). With most of the Corinthians, a selfish individualism undermined the purpose of spiritual gifts. God cannot be glorified when Christians use for themselves what God intended to bless the body.

Digging In

The third test of the use of the spiritual gift of tongues is "Does it engage the mind?" Praying or speaking in a tongue with no ability to understand what is said is useless, according to Paul. Four times in

1 Corinthian 13:14–19 he uses the word "understanding," adding a greater rhetorical weight to the word every time he writes it. If the Holy Spirit gives someone the gift of tongues, Paul encourages that person to pray for the ability to interpret and understand what he or she is saying (14:13). Otherwise, even though one's spirit might be active, one's mind is disengaged and therefore "unfruitful." Paul has no category for the spirit divorced from the mind. In 14:32, he will argue the same for prophecy when he insists that "the prophets' spirits are subject to the prophets."

For the apostle, the Christian faith is very much a matter of mental discipline under the leading and empowering of the Holy Spirit. A quick survey of Paul's epistles reveals a vast vocabulary of mental activity: "Consider yourselves dead to sin . . ." (Rom. 6:11); "Dwell on these things . . ." (Phil. 4:8); "Take every thought captive . . ." (2 Cor. 10:5); "Set your minds on things above . . ." (Col. 3:2); "Be transformed by the renewing of your mind . . ." (Rom. 12:2). Over and over he instructs his converts and congregations to use their minds as instruments of righteousness that they might live on the earth as God has indeed declared them in heaven. Paul cannot conceive of a Christian activity that does not involve and stimulate a sanctified mind, especially the use of spiritual gifts.

Paul sees a ready solution for the conundrum. He will pray with *both* his mind and spirit, the same way he sings (1 Cor. 14:15). He need not employ any language he does not understand when God has given him a perfectly good one that he does. The problem is not speaking in tongues *per se*. Paul was even grateful that he spoke in tongues more than any of the Corinthians (14:18), but he *never* used it in any way that was separated from comprehension and appreciation of what he was communicating (14:19). He was even more adamant in terms of public expression. It would be better to say five words that others understand than ten thousand words in a language that no one else could comprehend.

Paul's final test of the gift of tongues is "Does it evangelize the lost?" This test is perhaps the most devastating to the Corinthian practice. To begin this part of his argument, Paul quotes from the prophet Isaiah, specifically 18:11–12 in which God, through his prophet, tells his people that since they have not listened to him through his prophets, now they will listen to him through the language of their Assyrian invaders (14:21). Paul uses this historical reference to make the case that God uses other languages for a sign, particularly to "unbelievers." Prophecy, on the other hand, is for those who believe (14:22).

The unequivocal statement, "Speaking in other tongues, then, is intended as a sign, not for believers but for unbelievers," negates the motive of edifying oneself. When the gift of tongues is used as it was on the day of Pentecost in Acts 2 and at the house of Cornelius in Acts 10, it has an evangelistic purpose. The gift of tongues was given as a means of proclamation and affirmation. Tongues had a dual missiological purpose of sharing the gospel with people of other language groups as well as confirming that this was indeed God's work.

The Corinthian church, however, had not used the gift of tongues to reach others. In fact, Paul even suggests that if unbelievers should come to their gatherings and hear so many simultaneous languages being spoken, they would think them "out of your minds" (14:23). Prophecy, on the other hand, was God imparting instruction and encouragement through prophets because the Word was not yet complete, and people did not have the New Testament writings. When prophets spoke the words God had given them, conviction and comfort resulted as God confirmed his word and people proclaimed, "God is really among you" (14:24–25).

Living It Out

The Spirit brings conviction, not confusion. If any use of tongues distracts from evangelism and edification or rejoices in a feeling rather than in the gospel and its transforming power, then it cannot be the kind of tongues encouraged in the New Testament. Instead, it falls into the category of tongues that Paul was correcting in this epistle. The simple rule Paul gives the church is that tongues should only be used when someone can understand them. We must ask if our claim to use the gifts genuinely causes unbelievers to "worship God, proclaiming, 'God is really among you'" (14:25).

God may still give the gift of tongues today, but if he does it will be in a context by which he allows someone to proclaim the gospel in a language that he or she has never studied in order to demonstrate his mighty power in the gospel and in miraculous gifting. Our love of the Holy Spirit demands we do nothing to devalue his marvelous work or to quench the Spirit, but neither should we attribute to him that which can easily be explained by human efforts.

Decently and in Order

1 Corinthians 14:26–40

The Big Picture

After reminding the Corinthians that love is the supreme gift and object of Christian desire, the single work of the Spirit that will last into eternity, Paul returned to his instruction about using the gifts. In 1 Corinthians 14:1–25 he explained the proper use of the gift of tongues and the superiority of the gift of prophecy because everyone can understand and be convicted by its message. In verses 26–40 his instruction broadens to include other gifts and practices, particularly their expression in the corporate worship service. Paul extends his consistent message that the gifts should serve the body rather than the individual to embrace other practices that have turned the corporate worship of the Corinthian church into a chaotic competition for control and self-aggrandizement.

Digging In

The church in which everyone leads is a church with no leader at all. In 1 Corinthians 14:26, Paul describes a church that has lost its sight of Christ. Nearly everyone wanted to do some public ministry, whether to sing a song, teach a lesson, deliver a word of revelation, speak in tongues, or interpret what someone else said. The goal was the exercise of personal freedom more than corporate edification, but Paul insisted that "everything must be done for building up" the body, not for showing off one's gifts or enjoying one's preferences.

Ironically, throughout Paul's epistles he displays an aversion to rules. His remedy for excess is usually a Spirit-led mental discipline of reckoning oneself dead to sin but alive unto God (Rom. 6:11) or setting one's mind on Christ and those things which are above (Col. 3:2). In this case, however, the Corinthians have shown no ability to apply self-restraint. They have, in fact, used the gifts of the Spirit to demonstrate a complete lack of self-control and moderation in their flesh. They have undermined God's gifts with their own agendas. Paul's response, therefore, is to lay down some definitive rules in verses 27–36.

If someone has the gift of tongues, they should do it "each in turn" (14:27), no more than three in any service (and two seems to be preferable!), and only when an interpreter is present. In the same way, no more than three who have the gift of prophecy should prophesy, and "others should evaluate" (14:29) to make sure that nothing that is inconsistent with God's revealed truth passes as divine revelation. If the Lord moves upon a prophet during the service, the other prophet who has been speaking should be silent and listen (14:30). Clearly, Paul's guidelines require humility and trust between those who are using their gifts.

By issuing regulations for the gifts of the Spirit, Paul nullifies any suggestion that the one using a spiritual gift enters some ecstatic state and loses control. That is typical of demon possession, but not Spirit-led worship. "The prophets' spirits are subject to the prophets" (14:32) means that anyone who has a spiritual gift will also have discernment about the proper time and place for its use. The purpose will always be edification and the context will always be the church body.

Not only had tongues and prophecy been abused in the church, but so had the newfound freedom the women had discovered since becoming Christians (14:33b–36). In the Greco-Roman world, women were not citizens, they could not vote and had very little place in public life. Jesus valued women (Luke 8:2–3, for example) and so did the early church. Paul's fond commendation of Phoebe and many other women in his farewell greetings of Romans 16 indicates the important role they served and the high esteem in which they were held.

Though Paul sees salvation as irrespective of gender (Gal. 3:28), he nonetheless maintains that it does not erase the distinctions God established in creation and reiterated after the fall (1 Tim. 2:8–15). Paul has already instructed the Corinthians to maintain the reality and the symbols of authority in the home and in the church (1 Cor. 11:2–16), and now he commands that the Corinthian women should reflect that order in worship. They could pray and prophesy so long as they displayed that authority by having their heads covered (11:5), but they were not allowed to speak *in an authoritative manner* as a pastor or elder. They were to "keep silent" and refrain from interruption (14:34) just as someone with the gift of tongues should "keep silent" when no interpreter was present (14:28) and someone who is prophesying when another person receives something from the Lord should then "be silent" (14:30).

The married women in the church were apparently interrupting with "questions," which were thinly disguised teaching, perhaps even directed at their own husbands in a humiliating way. He directs them to save their questions for their husbands at home rather than to speak and interrupt (14:35). By declaring that all the churches of God are in agreement on this issue (14:33), a fact which is no longer true, to say the least, the apostle suggests that the church at Corinth was out of step with the culture, with other churches, and with "the law" (14:34), probably a reference to the creation narrative in Genesis. Paul's meaning in verse 36 is that the church of Corinth does not have one truth while other churches have another. If the Word of God didn't come just to them or originate with them, they cannot practice something that is completely out of step with sister churches who follow the same Lord.

Paul was nothing if not supremely confident in his apostleship and discernment of the will of the Lord. Anyone who claims to be a prophet will assent to what he says because Paul received it from the Lord (14:37). Paul *knows* where his teaching came from, and he asserts that anyone who thinks differently "will be ignored" (14:38) because a contradiction in God's mind and subsequent revelation is inconceivable.

Despite all the chaos in the Corinthian believers' worship, Paul does not forbid the use of the gifts nor does he see that as an option for the church (14:39), but his summary conclusion of the matter is that all worship is done "decently and in order" (14:40).

Living It Out

Modern culture, especially in the West, emphasizes individuality and personal expression, sometimes to the point of idolatry. Feelings and fulfillment take precedence over the worship and adoration of Jesus. Churches have often exacerbated the situation by catering to personal preferences and demands rather than teaching that Christ, not Christians, is the focus of worship. Paul points believers to a life that is fulfilling not because of gifts, but because of the Spirit's work in bestowing and placing them where they are needed in shared ministry with others, that respects God's purpose in creation, in calling, and in the church. Giftedness without selflessness is meaningless.

The Definition of the Gospel

1 Corinthians 15:1–11

The Big Picture

After a protracted discourse on spiritual gifts in 1 Corinthians 12–14, Paul turns his attention to the heart and definition of the gospel because, as will become evident, some Corinthians are challenging the notion that Christians will be resurrected. Paul argues that the resurrection of Christians is inextricably connected to the resurrection of Jesus, and no doctrine is more central or essential to Christianity than the resurrection of Jesus. To deny one is to deny the other. Salvation does not come through his sinless life, or even through his sacrificial death alone, but through the resurrection, which indisputably attests to both. The resurrection testifies that God has accepted his sacrifice as the atonement for sin and that Jesus has conquered death for his people. First Corinthians 15 is the Bible's most developed theological explanation of Christ's resurrection and its centrality to the gospel as well as its effects for believers. In this final major section of the epistle, Paul places the keystone in the arch of Christian doctrine for the church in Corinth as well as all churches through succeeding ages. Nothing else of his teachings will ultimately matter if the doctrine of the resurrection is lost. Paul spends the first eleven verses of the chapter defining and defending the gospel and its essential nature.

Digging In

Christians face no greater question than "What is the gospel?" and fight no greater battle than the struggle to keep it at the center of the Christian faith. Many have offered anthropocentric definitions of the gospel that focus on moral reformation, cultural associations, or global transformation, but to redefine or to dilute the gospel is to lose it. Anything *close* to the gospel is *not* the gospel. What rings true is this clear, inspired, Christocentric definition that Paul "received" from the Lord (15:3), which he "preached to" the Corinthians (15:1), which they, in turn, "received" from him, and on which they had taken their stand: "that Christ died for our sins according to the Scriptures, that he was buried," and that "he was raised on the third day according to the Scriptures" (15:3–4).

This clarion declaration is carefully packed with life-giving truth, which merits equally careful exegetical contemplation. Paul begins this final crescendo of his theological epistle with the desire to "make clear . . . the gospel," because it is the means by which believers "are being saved," a progressive construction indicating that salvation is not yet completed; it has only begun. Salvation has three tenses. Believers may look back and accurately refer to the moment of the new birth in the past by saying, "I *was* saved." Elsewhere, Paul looks to the future final redemption with the encouraging truth that "we *will be* saved through him from wrath" (Rom. 5:19). In this context, Paul focuses on salvation's continuing present effects. Christians "*are being* saved" (also in 1 Cor. 1:18; 2 Cor. 2:15) from the power of sin and death every day as the Holy Spirit sanctifies and matures those who are united to Christ by faith. In the brief conditional phrase, "if you hold to the message I preached to you" (1 Cor. 15:2), Paul reminds the Corinthians of his warning in 1 Corinthians 9:27–10:13 that only those who persevere truly belong to Christ. In 1:8 he expressed his confidence in their ulti-mate salvation, writing, "He will also strengthen you to the end, so that you will be blameless in the day of our Lord Jesus Christ," In this passage, he balances that assurance with the possibility that *some* among them could be false professors. If they do not have a genuine faith of the heart that continues, then they only had an intellectual belief that was "in vain" (15:2).

Paul's emphasis on the death, burial, and resurrection of Jesus as the message of the gospel is amplified by his twice repeated phrase, "according to the Scriptures." The person, the purpose, and the prophecy of Jesus' resurrection make it completely unique. Lazarus, the brother of Mary and Martha, died, was buried, and was resurrected, but not "for our sins" nor "according to the Scriptures." Only Jesus' death, burial, and resurrection happened as the fulfillment of prophecies and for the removal of others' sins. Jesus explained this to the disciples on the road to Emmaus on the day of his resurrection "beginning with Moses and all the Prophets . . . the things concerning himself in all the Scriptures" that it was "necessary for the Messiah to suffer these things and to enter into his glory" (Luke 24:26–27). Jesus' burial is often the ignored part of the gospel, but even it was prophesied in Isaiah 53:9 that "He was assigned a grave with the wicked, but he was with a rich man at his death" (Isa. 53:9), which was fulfilled by his burial in Joseph of Arimathea's grave near Golgotha. Everything Jesus did had purpose and was according to God's plan.

In confirmation of the gospel's historicity Paul shares that the resurrected Christ appeared to Peter (Cephas) and the Twelve Apostles, and to a crowd of five hundred people at one time (15:5–6). When Paul wrote this letter to the Corinthians, probably in AD 53–54, many of those eyewitnesses were still alive and could verify this testimony. Jesus also appeared to his earthly brother, James, who had not previously believed in him (Mark 3:21). When he came face-to-face with his resurrected and glorified brother, he realized that Jesus was both Lord and Christ, giving the rest of his life to count himself "a servant of God and of the Lord Jesus Christ" (James 1:1). Just as Peter relates to the Twelve, James seems to emerge as the leader of the other "apostles," those who are sent by the church, and a key leader in the Jerusalem congregation (Acts 15:13–21).

The last person that Jesus physically appeared to was Paul on the road to Damascus, well after the ascension. Realizing the strangeness of this appearance, he characterizes it "as to one born at the wrong time." Though Paul never denies his apostolic authority and teaching, he exhibits a refreshing personal humility by suggesting that he is the "least of the apostles" and "not worthy" to be called one because of his murderous past as a relentless persecutor of the church. He sees Christ's call on his life, therefore, as a work of grace that motivates him to work harder for God than anyone, not because he has anything to prove but because he has been given so much. But the instrument God uses to bring the gospel, whether Paul or someone else, is irrelevant. What matters is that the gospel is proclaimed and "so you have believed." Their testimony of belief in Christ's resurrection is going to be the basis on which Paul asserts that they must, therefore, believe in the resurrection of all believers.

Living It Out

The resurrection of Jesus is what separates Christianity from all other religions, the historical fact on which we ground our present faith and future resurrection. Our hope is not in ourselves, but in God who raises the dead (2 Cor. 1:9)! If we ever relegate the resurrection to a mere leap of faith in the heart of the believer rather than to the historical act by which God raised his Son from the reality of death, we lose the gospel and the distinctiveness of Christian faith. To lose the gospel would be to lose everything.

The Centrality of the Resurrection

1 Corinthians 15:12–34

The Big Picture

In their correspondence with Paul, the Corinthian church had revealed that some among them challenged the belief that Christians who died would be raised in the resurrection. Chapter 15 in 1 Corinthians is Paul's unwavering rebuttal of that denial. In 15:1–11 he laid the groundwork by maintaining the historicity of Jesus' resurrection from the dead and its centrality to the gospel. In today's passage he takes the next step in his logic, reasoning that the resurrection of believers is inseparable from the resurrection of Christ. Because we are united to him in every way, what is true of Christ is true of the believer. Because he was raised, so will we be. The only way Christians would not be resurrected would be because God did not raise Jesus either. It cannot be true of one and not the other. If Jesus is not raised, then neither will we be, and there is no hope and we are eternally lost. Yet, on the contrary, everything Paul does and calls on his disciples to do bears witness to belief on the deepest level that Christ is raised and will raise us up with him at the last day.

Digging In

After arguing for the historicity of Christ's resurrection, Paul finds it stupefying that any member of the church at Corinth could claim "There is no resurrection of the dead." Though they probably meant only to deny that Christians are raised, Paul declares that to reject that is to reject the other. In verses 12–19, he follows this assertion to its hopeless logical conclusion. If the dead are not raised, then Christ wasn't either. If Christ wasn't raised, then our preaching and our faith is pointless. We are charlatans and liars because we preach a false gospel. Worst of all, no one has been forgiven of their sins, we are all still guilty, and those who have died have perished without hope. If Christ isn't raised, we are the most pitiable people on the planet because we have invested our lives in a complete falsehood.

One might wonder why Paul denies even the possibility that Jesus was resurrected but people will not be. Paul explains this precisely in verses 20–28, that the resurrection is one eschatological event that happens to every single person who ever walked on the earth, but it will occur in three stages "each in his own order" (15:23). The resurrection of Christ is the "firstfruits," the promise that more is to follow. Just as death came through one man, Adam, so also the resurrection comes through one man, Jesus Christ (15:21–22). The entire human race was in Adam and when he fell, all fell with him. Likewise, the new humanity was represented in Christ and when God raised him up, their eventual resurrection was guaranteed.

So, the three stages of the resurrection are first, the resurrection of Christ, then comes the second stage, "at his coming, those who belong to Christ" (15:23). This resurrection of the saved is the event described in Revelation 20:1–4. Paul does not mention how long the interim period is between the resurrection of Christ's people and the third, final stage, "the end, when he hands over the kingdom to God the Father" and puts all enemies under his feet, especially death, "the last enemy to be abolished" (1 Cor. 15:24–26). Revelation 20:5, however, states that this final stage of the resurrection when the unsaved are raised to judgment occurs after the period known as the "thousand years" (cf. Rev. 20:11–15). The significance of the final stage of the resurrection, in which the unjust are raised to judgment, is that Jesus will destroy all enemies, and everything will be put under his feet. Only then will Christ the conqueror, to whom all are subject, lovingly subject himself to the Father (1 Cor. 15:28).

In 1 Corinthians 15:29–34, Paul moves from a theological argument for the resurrection to a personal one. He is asking the Corinthians to examine their behavior, as well as his, in light of the resurrection. To paraphrase, Paul is asking, "Why would we do x if there is no resurrection?" His first example in 15:29 about those "who are being baptized for the dead" is notoriously difficult to interpret, and in a brief study such as this space is too limited to survey all the possible views. Let it suffice to say that this author believes that "the dead" Paul refers to consistently throughout the chapter (see 15:12 [2x], 13, 15, 16, 20, 21, 29 [2x], 32, 35, 42, 52)[17] are the righteous dead who will be raised to glory and whom the Corinthians desire to join as testified by their confession through baptism. Others who trusted Christ and "have fallen asleep in Christ" (15:18) have influenced them and now they have been baptized on account of them and their influence. Since the dead have influenced their baptism, Paul essentially is asking the Corinthians, "If you don't believe in the resurrection, why would you want to join their number? What advantage would that be?"

Finally, Paul holds up his own behavior to prove his bedrock belief in the resurrection. He risked his life daily to spread the gospel. He even fought wild beasts in Ephesus. Why would he lose the comforts of life and suffer so much pain and grief unless he were certain of the resurrection? Paul admits that hedonism would be the proper lifestyle if this life is all there is and ever will be (15:32). His reference to bad company that corrupts good morals in verse 33 suggests that Paul lays much of the blame for this doctrinal aberration at the feet of unnamed teachers who have led the Corinthians away. While that dynamic is at the heart of 2 Corinthians, here it remains an oblique suggestion hidden within a reminder to "come to your senses and stop sinning" (15:34). To their shame, their denial of the resurrection is nothing but an appalling ignorance about God. "He is not the God of the dead but of the living, because all are living to him" (Luke 20:38)!

Living It Out

While Christians sometimes exhibit an inordinate fascination with how and when the Bible's final prophecies will play out in fulfillment and Christ will return, Paul's concern is not primarily about the future but about the present. The great truth he wants his readers to comprehend is that *the resurrection has already begun*! The believer's future resurrection is guaranteed because Christ is the firstfruits, a fact securely pegged in history. Just as the believer has a righteousness that comes from Christ, so is the believer's resurrection inseparable from that of Jesus. Our hope is secure. We need not fret or worry, and we certainly should not live hedonistically as though this life is all we have. Eternity is ours and we should live secure in the knowledge that Christ was raised into glory—and we will be too!

Day Thirty-Seven

Raised in Glory

1 Corinthians 15:35–49

The Big Picture

First Corinthians 15 is Paul's extended presentation of the centrality of the resurrection to the Christian faith. Some members of the church at Corinth had denied the postmortem resurrection of believers, so Paul systematically answers their objections, insisting that the believer's resurrection is inseparable from the resurrection of Jesus. Part of the argument that Paul encountered was a sarcastic mockery of what a resurrection body would be like, as though the concept itself were self-contradictory. While Paul bristles at the tone he hears in the challenge, he devotes significant space in his letter to return a serious answer to a derisive question. In 15:35–49, Paul marshals arguments from God's acts in nature and in history to suggest the nature of a glorified, resurrected body.

Digging In

Paul's pen drips with the sarcastic tone of his imaginary "someone" (though he may know exactly which of the Corinthians would respond this way) who asks, "How are the dead raised? What kind of body will they have when they come?" (15:35). Just as Jesus charged the Emmaus disciples with being foolish and having hearts slow to believe the Scriptures (Luke 24:25), Paul's language reflects his frustration with the Corinthians' unbelief. Turning the normal way of thinking on its head, Paul claims that life follows death more than the other way around. The seed must die for the real life to begin, echoing the words of Jesus in John 12:24, "unless a grain of wheat falls to the ground and dies, it remains by itself. But if it dies, it produces much fruit." Paul sees death as the essential catalyst for resurrected life. Just as in agriculture, the seed does not necessarily look like the plant it produces, so the resurrection body will be very different from the body of this earth. Just as God gives each seed that is planted its own kind of body, so will he do for a resurrected body that springs from the corruptible body that was buried. Paul highlights both the sovereignty and the intimacy of God as he gives to each one "a body as he wants" (1 Cor. 15:38).

In verses 39–41, Paul is alluding to the creation passage in Genesis 1, specifically the kinds of animals or "flesh" God created on days six, five, and four. He did not create all animals with the same kind of flesh, so no one should assume that the resurrection body will be like what God has created previously. The same is true for the "earthly" and "heavenly" bodies that he made on the fourth day of creation. God gave to each one a different "splendor" or glory, revealing his boundless creativity and perfect administration of his creation. God's beauty and variety in creation is key to understanding the resurrection of those who will populate a new heaven and a new earth.

The one thing Paul makes clear is that the glorified resurrected body will be nothing like the one that was part of the fallen, broken world. It will be incorruptible, glorious, powerful, and "spiritual" (15:42–44), by which Paul does not mean that it is not corporeal, but rather that it will not be bound by the natural laws of decay and death. Paul had a distinct advantage in writing these words because he had seen and been in the presence of the glorified body of the risen Christ. Paul's concept of the resurrection body of believers surely springs from that encounter with "the life-giving spirit" (15:45), "the heavenly man" to whose "image" believers will conform (15:49).[18] The natural body springs from creation and is passed down genetically from Adam, but the spiritual body is animated and made possible by Christ's glorious resurrection.

One can feel the excited anticipation of Paul as he reflects on the glorified, spiritual body that awaits him. As he noted in Galatians 6:17, his earthly body bore scars, the "marks of Jesus" as a result of his suffering. He fought with wild beasts, he was stoned and left for dead and many other things that tore and scarred his body (2 Cor. 11:24–29). If anyone knew the limitations of an earthly body, Paul did. But he also knew that one day, in the not-too-distant future, his earthly body would be planted like a seed and, when it sprang forth in new life, he would bear the image of "the man of heaven" just as his earthly body had born the image of Adam, the man of dust. As he explained to the Philippians, in the resurrection Christ ". . . will transform the body of our humble condition into the likeness of his glorious body, by the power that enables him to subject everything to himself" (Phil. 3:21).

Living It Out

Belief in the resurrection does not merely provide comfort in the face of pain and relief from the fear of death, but a daily reminder that this life should not be the object of our love or the source of fear that we might lose it. Paul believed in the resurrection so much that he could fearlessly fight wild beasts at Ephesus—and, since he lived to write about it, apparently win! He had seen the resurrected Christ and he had confidence that his resurrected body is going to be far better, something incomparable to the body as it exists in this life.

The doctrine of the resurrection is not an academic theological construct that has no practical effect on us now. To the contrary, knowing that the resurrection has already begun because Christ arose, that our resurrection to glory is guaranteed by Christ, our Forerunner (Heb. 6:20), should make every Christian live fearlessly but soberly. We are fearless because we have a guarantee of glory, but we are sober and serious about life because this is our opportunity to make eternal investments with the gifts and moments God has given us.

The Last Trumpet

1 Corinthians 15:50–58

The Big Picture

Discovering that some of the members of the Corinthian church doubted the resurrection must have brought sorrow to Paul's heart. No doctrine is more central to Christian faith than the bodily resurrection of Jesus, and its loss means the loss of the gospel. For this reason, the great apostle spent much time and ink carefully making the case for the historicity of Jesus' resurrection followed by a lengthy list of its implications for all believers. His primary assertion is that the resurrection of Jesus is the "firstfruits" of the resurrection and has two stages yet to come. The second stage is the resurrection of believers at the return of Christ that results in a glorified body, and the third stage is the resurrection of unbelievers to judgment, which Paul calls "the end, when he hands over the kingdom to God the Father" and abolishes death itself (1 Cor. 15:23–28). After explaining the glory of the resurrection body and its radical difference from the natural body in this life, Paul arrives at the apex of his resurrection discourse. In verses 50–58, he provides some sense of the sequence, if not the timing, of how this change will occur in conjunction with Christ's return, and of the marvelous victory that Christ accomplishes in the resurrection of his people. His final appeal is that the knowledge of this complete and ultimate victory should shape the daily lives of believers and motivate them to be steadfast in their labor for the Lord.

Digging In

The details about the transformation of the resurrection body have been startling; but rather than moderating his explanation, Paul highlights the distinction between the now and then with the stark declaration that "flesh and blood cannot inherit the kingdom of God." Lest his readers think of the resurrection body as simply an extension of this life into eternity, Paul describes the age to come as fundamentally different from this age, therefore so must be the bodies that dwell there. God is not just making this world better; he's making a new world. Likewise, he is not making Christian bodies healthier or more durable, he's making them incorruptible and indestructible. They will not be of flesh and blood that has characterized the broken lives on this fallen planet. They will be "clothed" with incorruptibility and immortality. Just as Paul explained in the beginning of his epistle that a person without the Spirit cannot receive what comes from God's Spirit (2:14), now he reveals that the person characterized by the flesh of this world cannot inherit a spiritual kingdom. The body that comes from Adam is corruptible because of sin and it cannot "inherit incorruption" (15:50).

How will this marvelous change take place? Paul answers that this is a mystery. For Paul the word *mystery* has a precise, almost technical, meaning. A mystery is something that was previously hidden, but now, in the new covenant, has been revealed in the person and the work of Christ. A mystery is not something that readers need to figure out, but something the Holy Spirit has already revealed to New Testament believers. The Holy Spirit has now disclosed that the change will be instantaneous at the return of Christ, and it will happen to two groups of people: those who have "fallen asleep," or died in Christ, and those who are alive and "changed" (15:51). The Old Testament spoke of the Kingdom and described many ways that the people of God would enjoy it: peace, a reversal of the curse, a restoration of fellowship, and the presence of God, for instance. In this passage, however, Paul reveals something that has never been previously known: though all believers will not die, all must be changed from corruptible bodies to incorruptible ones. The return of Christ will signal a complete transformation as the mortal is "clothed" with immortality and the corruptible is "clothed" with incorruption. We have worn the "clothes" of Adam, but we finally will be clothed in the likeness of Christ!

This radical reordering of the world and of the bodies of believers will not be gradual or imperceptible, but sudden—"in a moment, in the twinkling of an eye"—and unmistakable—"at the last trumpet" when "the dead will be raised incorruptible" (15:52). Whether the believer's body is alive at the moment of Christ's return or has been buried in the earth does not alter the outcome at all: "we will all be changed" and share in Christ's victory over death.

Fittingly, Paul's description of the resurrection reaches a crescendo in a song of fulfillment taken from similar prophetic passages in the Old Testament. "Death has been swallowed up in victory" (15:54) alludes to Isaiah 25:8, "When he has swallowed up death once and for all, the Lord GOD will wipe away the tears from every face and remove his people's disgrace." "Where, death, is your victory? Where, death, is your sting?" (1 Cor. 15:55) refers to Hosea 13:14, which reads in part, "I will ransom them from the power of Sheol. I will redeem them from death. Death, where are your barbs? Sheol, where is your sting?" The meaning of both references is clear. The "sting" or "barb" of death is sin, and sin is only powerful and able to condemn because of the law, but the Lord Jesus Christ vanquishes them both and the resurrected body of the believer is subject to neither (1 Cor. 15:57). The disgrace and sorrow of death will be completely eradicated by the triumph of Christ.

Paul always lands his theology in Christian conduct. His eschatology leads to sanctification. Verse 58 is the duty after the doctrine. Any believer who understands that the resurrection of Christ guarantees the resurrection of his followers should live steadfastly, unmoved by the calamities, difficulties, and circumstances of this world. A knowledge of future transformation should result in a transformed life right now. All "labor in the Lord is not in vain" (15:58) but will be recorded and rewarded by the One in whose work we always excel.

Living It Out

Understanding that Christ has defeated sin and set aside the law prevents a Christian from being a pessimist who does not believe in the resurrection (as in 15:12), a hedonist who believes this life is all that matters (as in 15:32), or a fatalist who docilely surrenders to circumstances and does not excel in the work of the Lord (as admonished in 15:58). The resurrection is not only a soothing comfort, but also an encouraging motivation. The follower of Jesus does not fight *for* victory but *from* victory because Christ has won it! Though all believers will be changed at the last trumpet in a moment, the knowledge of the resurrection changes us even now.

Effective Ministry, Great Opposition

1 Corinthians 16:1–12

The Big Picture

In the final section of his first epistle, Paul ties up several loose ends and gives final instructions to the Corinthians. After the lofty prose and deep eschatology, beyond the disclosure of mysteries and the revelations of the resurrection, are the practical concerns about receiving an offering, where to spend the winter, and how to treat a young minister. In a span of a few words, Paul moves from the glory of the resurrection body and Christ's defeat of death to the mundane matters that any church must face. This chapter is a reminder that theology is to be lived, not merely learned.

Digging In

Three times in this letter, in 1 Corinthians 7:1, 16:1, and 16:12, Paul takes up a subject that the Corinthian church and he have already communicated about by using the phrase, "Now about . . ." The change would not seem so abrupt to the original audience who had knowledge of previous correspondence or conversations. In the first verse of the chapter, he turns their attention to the offering for the church in Jerusalem, apparently because they have been hard hit by a famine and perhaps persecution. Paul was asking churches around the Mediterranean to send help back to the mother church (see Rom. 15:25–32; Acts 24:17; 2 Cor. 8–9).

Paul's instructions in 1 Corinthians 16:1–3 present several principles of giving that, though specifically written to the church at Corinth, are helpful guidelines for all believers. First, giving is to be regular, in this case weekly. The church gathered "on the first day of the week" in commemoration of the resurrection, and that was the natural time for the members to give their offering. Second, it was to be personal. "*Each of you* is to set something aside" (v. 2, italics added). Third, it was to be proportional. Each giver should make a gift "in keeping with how he is prospering." Paul was not demanding a set amount that would be too great a burden for the poorer members and hardly generous at all for the wealthier members. Though the Old Testament prescribes a tithe, ten percent, as a proportion, Paul does not mention a set percentage. He simply suggests that it should be based on one's own level of prosperity so that, while the gifts may not be equal, the level of generosity should be. Fourth, the offering was protracted. Paul was not satisfied with a single offering hastily collected just before his arrival. He knew that would mean less money and less intention on the part of the church. The offering should be collected over the course of weeks and months and kept until his arrival. Finally, their offering should be protected. They should safeguard all of it until the apostle's arrival, and then they can send the offering with reputable members to deliver it to the Jerusalem saints along with letters of introduction from Paul. Paul even notes that he might be able to join them for the journey.

When Paul introduces the possibility that he might travel to Jerusalem with representatives from Corinth, he turns his attention to travel possibilities for the future (16:5–9). Reading Paul's potential travel plans allows insight into his personal life that are not as visible in the more formal parts of his letters, particularly how he conceptualizes the power of his personal presence and relationships. Travel in the ancient world was difficult, often treacherous. To get to Corinth, Paul would have taken a combination of land and sea travel and the journey would have taken months (see Acts 17:13–18:1 for the route Paul took on his first journey to Corinth). The clear picture that emerges is that the future for Paul is not entirely clear. In other words, God's will was not a tantalizing point for which Paul must aim but rather a divine purpose that shaped decisions as they presented themselves. Paul was not asking, "Does God want me to stay in Corinth for the winter or not?" He was committed to whatever "advanced the gospel" (Phil. 1:12). Every travel decision was based on how he could best do that. Sometimes the Lord did not allow his plans to be realized (such as in Acts 16:7), and Paul trusted that the Lord would always lead him in whatever way best realized his goal.

Paul knew that personal presence deepens relationships in ways that correspondence cannot. Whether visiting the churches in Macedonia or spending the winter in Corinth, Paul used his presence to point people to Christ. He had a desire to "spend some time" with his beloved Corinthian converts, not "just in passing" but in a way that bound their ties more tightly. Yet even his good desires with good intentions and godly purposes might give way to something better that he could not yet see, so he tempered his plans with the humility and the phrase, "if the Lord allows."

Most striking in this section is the contrast between opportunity, "a wide door for effective ministry has opened for me," and opposition, "yet many oppose me." Ephesus was a major seaport and, therefore, a key position from which the gospel could spread. The metropolis fit Paul's evangelistic strategy perfectly. According to Acts 18:19–21, Paul arrived there during his second missionary journey and returned to it on his third (Acts 19:1–20). Yet, with this opportunity came great opposition. Paul even nearly lost his life there (Acts 19:23–41). The will of God cannot be determined by the ease with which doors open or results happen.

Finally, in 1 Corinthians 16:10–11 Paul admonishes the Corinthians to receive and respect Timothy, his young protégé. He has already mentioned him in 4:17 as "my dearly loved and faithful child in the Lord" and informed the church that he is coming to "remind you of my ways in Christ Jesus." His importance to Paul is reiterated through using some of his final words of this to ensure that Timothy "has nothing to fear while with you." Paul knew how hard and hurtful ministry can sometimes be, especially in a church so fractured and doctrinally confused, and he wanted to spare his son in the faith having anyone "look down on him." Perhaps Paul felt the need to protect Timothy because he knew that the Corinthians would be disappointed to learn that Apollos, whom many of the members followed (1:12; 3:4–6), would not be coming. Whatever the reasons, Paul's care for his son in the faith and desire to receive him back is a beautiful demonstration of paternal care for a younger minister.

Living It Out

This passage is saturated with a concern for others and a deep desire to do the will of God. In every relationship, Paul points others to Christ and to holiness. The motive of every action and every plan should be to do all to the glory of God. Whenever we make doing the will of God our goal, God will always give us a way to bring glory to him, whether through relationships, travel, work, or even opposition.

Firm in the Faith

1 Corinthians 16:13–24

The Big Picture

Paul concludes his letter with instructions and greetings that follow the theological and corrective movements of the letter. Pastoral, even parental, in tone, Paul sounds these staccato notes of admonition to bring his epistle to a close after the great resurrection crescendo of 1 Corinthians 15. Though the tone and the tenor of chapter 16 are noticeably different, the theme perfectly reflects his insistence that the proper response to understanding the resurrection is "always [to be] excelling in the Lord's work" (15:58), which is precisely what Paul models and in his concluding encouragement to his beloved Corinthians.

Digging In

In two verses, Paul delivers five imperatives that reiterate much of his teaching from the first fifteen chapters (16:13–14). He sounds like a parent giving final instructions to his child at the door or an officer addressing soldiers just before battle. They need to be "alert" to the insidious influences around them that have crept into the church and influenced their thinking. They must "stand firm in the faith" rather than to be blown around by every wind of teaching. Living as Christians in a pagan culture requires that they "be courageous," in the face of the world's opposition. Obedience to the truth, especially a readiness to surrender one's own rights, can only be achieved by the "strong." Though it may lack the sublime poetry, "Do everything in love" is a succinct and accurate summary of chapter 13 and the remedy for most of the church's division. In fact, had the Corinthians genuinely lived by these five imperatives, they would not have needed much of Paul's correction from the preceding fifteen chapters.

One of the members whom the Corinthian church had sent to Paul bearing their correspondence was Stephanas, whose household, Paul reminds them, was "the firstfruits of Achaia" (16:15). Not only were they some of the first converts, but the image of "firstfruits" invokes the picture of an offering of the early harvest that indicated more to come. Stephanas must have trusted Christ when Paul arrived in Corinth toward the end of his second missionary journey (Acts 18:1–11). Paul noted that he showed an inclination and devotion "to serving the saints." Paul believed that his disposition to serve qualified him to lead, so he urges the church to "submit to such people, and to everyone who works and labors with them" (1 Cor. 16:16), a strong suggestion that they mark him as a leader and follow him accordingly.

Paul's declaration of delight at the presence of Stephanas, Fortunatus, and Achaicus is an expression of gratitude, a reminder that Christian fellowship brings joy. If he could not be with the entire church, at least he could be with these three men who carried greetings and news and, in some measure, "made up for" the absence of the church. Their arrival in Ephesus "refreshed" Paul's spirit and, as a result, they had the same effect on their fellow church members, too. These men, particularly Stephanas, were model church members with servant hearts and a refreshing manner. Paul marks them as worthy of leadership and recognition (16:18). To a church that had valued giftedness over godliness, this was particularly pointed.

Writing from Ephesus, Paul had contact with many other churches and Christians from whom he sends greetings as well. Throughout the epistle, Paul has mentioned "other churches" when he was instructing the Corinthians in some controversial matters (7:17; 11:16; 14:33–34; 16:1), no doubt to remind them that they are part of something larger than themselves and accountable to others in their stand for truth. This final reference to "the churches of Asia" drives the point home.

Aquila and Priscilla were well known to the church in Corinth. Paul met them when he first arrived there (Acts 18:1–2) and since they shared the tentmaking trade, the three of them worked together. Leaving Corinth for Syria eighteen months later, he took them along, but then left them in Ephesus while he continued to his destination (Acts 18:18–21). When Apollos came to Ephesus, Aquila and Priscilla discovered him teaching and discerned that he was mighty in the Scriptures, but also knew that he needed to be taught "the way of God more accurately" (Acts 18:26), so they discipled him. Apollos obviously had a prominent role in the church at Corinth, largely due to the influence of this devout couple. Not only do they send greetings, but also "the church that meets in their home," indicating their continued influence and the common bond these two churches shared.

"All the brothers and sisters" (1 Cor. 16:20) suggests that Ephesus, a very large city geographically, had more churches than the one that met in Aquila and Priscilla's home, and Paul was in contact with all of them. With the greetings, he includes an encouragement to mutual affection, to "greet one another with a holy kiss." No explanation accompanies this mandate because it was the common practice of that time and place. Paul emphasizes, however, that it should be a "holy" kiss, which qualifies both the intent and the action and is especially warranted in a church characterized by conflict.

Paul's final words in verses 21–24 are written in his own hand rather than by his amanuensis, probably Sosthenes (1:1). The last three verses each refer to Jesus in some form, hardly surprising for a letter whose first three verses mentioned Jesus as well and whose contents have consistently argued for the centrality of Christ. As always, Paul divides the world between those who know and love Christ as recipients of his grace, and those who do not love him, and are cursed. These two groups ultimately will be separated at the Lord's return, for which Paul prays (16:22). Appropriately, his last sentence conveys his love in Christ Jesus, which is both the reason for and the substance of his letter.

Living It Out

For all the complicated, chaotic problems of the Corinthian church, the solution Paul offers comes down to the grace of Christ and the selflessness of love. That's all we have, too. Without Christ, we cannot know truth, but without love, truth becomes a club we wield rather than a balm we apply. To be genuinely alert, firm in the faith, courageous, and strong, we must "do everything in love." Like Stephanas, we must serve others before we aspire to lead. Like Aquila and Priscilla, we must learn before we dare to teach. We must desire to be recognized for refreshing others by our presence instead of impressing them with our gifts. Living in love that manifests itself in service, we'll do everything for the glory of Christ instead of the promotion of self. Our Lord, come!

Notes

1. Lohannes P. Louw and Eugene A. Nida, *Greek-English Lexicon of the New Testament Based on Semantic Domains* (New York: United Bible Societies, 1989), 1:340.

2. Paul Ellingworth and Howard Hatton, *A Translator's Handbook on Paul's First Letter to the Corinthians* in the Helps for Translators series (London: United Bible Societies, 1985), 17.

3. W. W. Wiersbe, *The Bible Exposition Commentary*, vol. 1 (Wheaton, IL: Victor Books, 1996), 573.

4. George Eldon Ladd, *The Gospel of the Kingdom* (Grand Rapids, MI: Eerdmans, 1959), 52.

5. For a representative survey of the term *day*, see Isaiah 2:12; 3:18; 4:2; 13:6–22; Jeremiah 46:10; Ezekiel 7:19; 13:5; 30:1–3; Hosea 9:5; Joel 1:15; 2:1, 11, 31; Joel 3:14–21; Amos 5:18–20; Obadiah 1:15; Zephaniah 1:7–18; Zechariah 14:1–21; Malachi 4:1–6.

6. See Romans 13:12; 1 Corinthians 1:8; 4:5; 2 Corinthians 5:10; 1 Thessalonians 5:4; 2 Thessalonians 1:7–10; 2 Timothy 1:12, 18, 4:8.

7. John MacArthur, *1 Corinthians* in The MacArthur New Testament Commentary (Chicago, IL: Moody Press, 1984), 87–93.

8. R. E. Ciampa and B. S. Rosner, *The First Letter to the Corinthians* (Grand Rapids, MI; Cambridge, U.K.: William B. Eerdmans Publishing Company, 2010), 176.

9. Simon J. Kistemaker, *New Testament Commentary: Exposition of the First Epistle to the Corinthians* (Grand Rapids, MI: Baker Books, 1993), 138.

10. Ben Witherington III, *Conflict and Community in Corinth: A Socio-Rhetorical Commentary on 1 and 2 Corinthians* (Grand Rapids, MI: Wm. B. Eerdmans Publishing Co., 1995), 157.

11. Ibid., 160.

12. Ibid., 165.

13. Ciampa and Rosner, *The First Letter to the Corinthians*, 298.

14. L. P. Louw and E. A. Nida, *Greek-English Lexicon of the New Testament: Based on Semantic Domains* (electronic ed. of the 2nd edition., vol. 1) (New York: United Bible Societies, 1996), 738.

15. Ibid.

16. C. S. Lewis, *The Four Loves* (New York: Harcourt Brace, 1960), 155.

17. Ciampa and Rosner, *The First Letter to the Corinthians*, 783.

18. Ibid., 809.

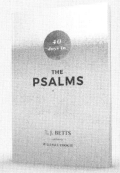